Married Couples
HIERARCHY
OF NEEDS

A Practical and Common Sense Guide
for Married Couples

C. S. GAFFNEY

Married Couples HIERARCHY OF NEEDS

A Book designed to Illustrate Essential Needs
That is Present in Successful Marriages

C.S. Gaffney
Author and Marriage Counselor

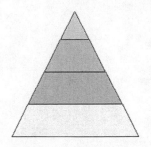

Order this book online at www.trafford.com
or email orders@trafford.com

Most Trafford titles are also available at major online book retailers.

© Copyright 2013 C.S. Gaffney.
All rights reserved. No part of this publication may be reproduced, stored in a retrieval system, or transmitted, in any form or by any means, electronic, mechanical, photocopying, recording, or otherwise, without the written prior permission of the author.

Printed in the United States of America.

ISBN: 978-1-4669-8367-0 (sc)
ISBN: 978-1-4669-8369-4 (hc)
ISBN: 978-1-4669-8368-7 (e)

Library of Congress Control Number: 2013904169

Trafford rev. 03/12/2013

 www.trafford.com

North America & international
toll-free: 1 888 232 4444 (USA & Canada)
phone: 250 383 6864 ♦ fax: 812 355 4082

Acknowledgments

Our natural conception and birth is a result of human cooperation and established the priority the Creator places on our dependency on others for success and personal progress. This work is evidence to this collaboration and substantiates the reality that we are a sum total of all the influences made to our lives by the people we have had the privilege to come across on the journey of life. I am deeply appreciative for the inspiration and wisdom of the men and women, both past and present, which, through their lives, instructions, corrections, challenges, commitment, and example, disturbed gifts within me that I did not know existed.

I am also grateful to all the friends and colleagues of the Church and Community, those military and corporate leaders who continue to inspire me to make a contribution to my generation and those to come.

For the development and production of this book itself, I feel a deep sense of gratitude to: My precious wife, Doris, and our children, Gary, Neressa, Sheryl and Jeff for their patience and support during my Military years. Being your husband and father tested the reality of the principles in this book and has made me an unquestionable husband and father. I love you all.

I am appreciative of my True Vine COGIC family and especially Superintendent Leo C. Brown Jr. the pastor who gave me an opportunity to oversee the marriage ministry of the church. It was through this ministry that provides me an unbeliever insight of how marriages work.

Introduction

Winifred Gaffney, my deceased mother for believing in me even when I doubted myself. Her intrinsic ability to help others was among the greatest contributions she implanted into me. Thanks Mom, without your earlier intervention there is a possibility this book would not exist.

The purpose of this book is to provide couples with a common sense approach of how to discover, and then understand how to meet, each other's most important emotional needs. When you were first married, you assumed that those needs would be met, but for a variety of reasons, you become very disillusioned . . . perhaps disillusioned enough to be enticed to let someone else meet your needs.

Usually ignorance contributes to this failure because men and women have great difficulty understanding and appreciating the value of each other's needs. Men tend to try to meet needs that they would value and women do the same. But the needs of men and women are often very different and by wasting effort trying to meet the wrong needs, a couple fails to make each other happy.

Husbands' and wives' needs are so strong that when they're not met in marriage, people are tempted to go outside marriage to satisfy them. And most of the people I've counseled have yielded to the temptation to violate their sacred vow to "forsake all others."

In his influential paper of 1943, *A Theory of Human Motivation*, the American psychologist Abraham Maslow proposed that healthy human beings have a certain number of needs, and that these needs are arranged in a hierarchy, with some needs (such as physiological and safety needs) being more primitive or basic than others (such as social and ego needs). Maslow's so-called 'hierarchy of needs' is often presented as a five-level pyramid, with higher needs coming into focus only when the lower and more basic needs are met.

The hierarchy of needs are also present in married couples needs as well. Maslow's theory was focused on individual needs to survive in this high pressure society. However when you look at successful marriages there was some essential needs that were present and priortised in a manner similar to Maslow's theory on the hierachy of needs.

As difficult as marriage can be to achieve, it is not complicated. And so, if I can't describe it in a page or two, then I've probably made it too complex. The true measure of a successful marriage is that it accomplishes the results that it sets out to achieve. To do that on a consistent, ongoing basis, a married couple must meet the five functional needs that are essential to a successful marriage. I am a great fan and follower of 'Patrick Lencioni" in is his book on the "Five Dysfunctions of a Team which align with my hierarchy of functional needs. I borrowed his model to further explain my functional of needs model. This book will show how those five functions play a major role in successful marriage.

The changing of society has also altered the family dynamic tremulously. Since both members of the married couple are working full time and often the same hours, the household chores and many other tasks have deviated from the traditional "his duties and her duties". This change has created conflict and disagreements. "Who does the household chores"? This topic will be discussed in the Common Sense Chapter.

You are capable of achieving more than you ever imagined by accessing the power that the Lord God has designed especially for you. His master plan is to carry you to new and exciting heights of splendor, hope, and love.

When economic troubles, family struggles, political upheavals, and natural disasters take center stage, you can rest assured with an inner peace that passes all understanding, that you have the power to victoriously live through it all. You are the salt of the earth, the beacon in a dark world, the refreshing stream for a thirsty land.

There's more to being in love than making each other happy, however. You must also know how to avoid making each other unhappy. That's why I've written this common sense book to aid in avoiding these states of unhappiness. Spouses can learn to become each other's source of greatest pleasure when they meet each other's most important emotional needs. On the contrary they can also become each other's source of unbearable pain when they don't protect each other from instincts and habits that are common to all of us.

MARRIED COUPLES HIERARCHY OF NEEDS

As you explore this book get ready to experience a new joy and strength that will change your life as you overcome adversity, succeed in achieving your goals, thrive in all aspects of your life, advance your dreams and visions, and win each race that you run with the help you will gain.

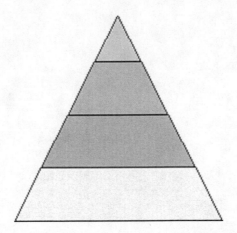

Chapter 1

Hierarchy of Needs

Married Couple Hierarchy of Needs

In his influential paper of 1943, *A Theory of Human Motivation*, the American psychologist Abraham Maslow proposed that healthy human beings have a certain number of needs, and that these needs are arranged in a hierarchy, with some needs (such as physiological and safety needs) being more primitive or basic than others (such as social and ego needs). Maslow's so-called 'hierarchy of needs' is often presented as a five-level pyramid, with higher needs coming into focus only when the lower and more basic needs are met.

The hierarchy of needs are also present in married couples needs as well. Maslow's theory was focused on individual needs to survive in this high pressure society. However when you look at successful marriages there was some essential needs that were present and priortised in a manner similar to Maslow's theory on the hierachy of needs.

Maslow called the bottom four levels of the pyramid 'deficiency needs' because a person does not feel anything if they are met, but becomes anxious if they are not. Thus, physiological needs such as eating, drinking, and sleeping are deficiency needs, as are safety needs, social needs such as friendship and sexual intimacy, and ego needs such as self-esteem and recognition. In contrast, Maslow called the fifth level of the pyramid a 'growth need' because it enables a person to 'self-actualize' or reach his fullest potential as a human being. Once a person has met his deficiency needs, he can turn his attention to self-actualization; however, only a small minority of people is able to self-actualize because self-actualization requires uncommon qualities such as honesty, independence, awareness, objectivity, creativity, and originality.

How a Couple Marriage Needs relates to needs defined by Maslow?

The first question we should examine in order to develop this belief of *Married Couples Hierarchy of Needs.* The assumptions of this writer are couples that are reading this material are Christians or believers in Biblical principles of marriage according to God's design for marriages:

In that view each marriage should begin with the scripture cited in Genesis 2:18-24.

> [18] And the Lord God said, it is not good that the man should be alone; I will make him an help meet for him.
>
> [19] And out of the ground the Lord God formed every beast of the field and every fowl of the air; and brought them unto Adam to see what he would call them: and whatsoever Adam called every living creature that was the name thereof.
>
> [20] And Adam gave names to all cattle and to the fowl of the air, and to every beast of the field; but for Adam there was not found an help meet for him.
>
> [21] And the Lord God caused a deep sleep to fall upon Adam, and he slept: and he took one of his ribs, and closed up the flesh instead thereof;
>
> [22] And the rib, which the Lord God had taken from man, made he a woman, and brought her unto the man.
>
> [23] And Adam said this is now bone of my bones, and flesh of my flesh: she shall be called Woman, because she was taken out of Man.
>
> [24] Therefore shall a man leave his father and his mother, and shall cleave unto his wife: and they shall be one flesh. **(KJV)"**

The second important scriptures in the marriages are those referenced in Ephesians 5:21-25 **(KJV).**

> [21] Submitting yourselves one to another in the fear of God.
>
> [22] Wives, submit yourselves unto your own husbands, as unto the Lord.
>
> [23] For the husband is the head of the wife, even as Christ is the head of the church: and he is the saviour of the body.
>
> [24] Therefore as the church is subject unto Christ, so let the wives be to their own husbands in everything.

> [25] Husbands, love your wives, even as Christ also loved the church, and gave himself for it.

The scriptures above describe and mandate two important needs within the married hierarchy of needs; **Love and Commitment.**

Hierarchy of Needs

Just how does a marriage survive? What must be present for both spouses to feel safe? How do both get their love needs fulfill? The same questions may be asked as to how both people get their esteem and actualization needs satisfied within the marriage.

While some of the answers may differ from couple to couple, there are basic qualities of marriage that most people in most cultures would agree must be present. By way of introduction, the Marital Hierarchy of Needs breaks down as follows:

Marriage Survival Needs: You must be legally married (in the eyes of the State or Church), have a mutual agreement to be married, live in the same house or at least have regular contact with your spouse. You must have Love, Respect, Trust, and Commitment. The Bible really defines commitment in Genesis 2:24 when it states: *"**Therefore shall a man leave his father and his mother, and shall cleave unto his wife: and they shall be one flesh"**.* Also in Ephesians 5:24 talks about this love need; *"**Husbands, love your wives, even as Christ also loved the church, and gave himself for it"**.*

From a financial standpoint, satisfying the Level 1 survival needs involves a wage earner's ability to meet the fundamental needs of food, clothing, and shelter—the basic needs of the family.

Unfortunately, far too many couples treat the monies allocated for food as a flexible part of the family budget that can be thought of as the "Peter" that can be robbed to pay "Paul" when money gets tight. As a consequence, many families, especially low—and fixed-income families, tend to buy food with the money that is left over after paying the rent, utilities, and other fixed bills such as car loans and monthly payments on credit cards.

From a hierarchical perspective, however, many of these contractual debts are acquired in an attempt to satisfy needs from a level higher than survival needs. According to Maslow, the higher levels should not be addressed until after the survival needs are satisfied. It is important that marriage partners recognize such discrepancies when they are setting up priorities regarding the allocation of resources. Basically, they are being asked to recognize the unreasonableness of buying a new microwave oven (because everyone has one) and then, because of the payments, being unable to buy food to cook in it.

Providing adequate food for the family is paramount to the family's physiological and psychological well-being.

Marriage Safety Needs: To feel safe with each other, you take care of and provide comfort to one another, create a home, have **financial security**, mutual trust, and honesty, protect one another physically, mentally and emotionally, and create an abuse-free environment within the marriage.

The primary challenge facing married couples in meeting their safety needs is knowing what they fear and whether or not these fears are based on reality or just imagined. Safety needs deal primarily with providing direct and indirect protection of oneself, loved ones, and property. In a direct sense, families face the problem of acquiring adequate protection against disease, accident, and crime as well as the need to provide adequate security for their property and assets.

For most families, property and assets translate into what the family calls "home." Being able to come up with the rent, build a house, or pay the mortgage is often paramount to maintaining a sense of well-being. How safe a family is from being evicted or how likely the couple will face a foreclosure is often directly related to the amount of income that the couple is able to earn compared to the size of their indebtedness.

Marriage Love Needs: Mutual love is an obvious requirement to have a marriage that operates from this level. Kindnesses, compassion, companionship, intimacy, affection, sex (love-making) are also important factors.

To meet one's love needs, a person must first feel safe enough to love without demanding reciprocation. If an individual loves someone and that person rejects this love or fails to love back, that person has—tragically—missed an opportunity to experience being loved.

Unfortunately, in many marriages, love is seen as a commodity that can be bought, sold, and exchanged for goods and services. As a consequence, a great many marriages have ended in financial disaster due to attempts at buying love. In such instances, there is a tendency to substitute gifts for feelings and to substitute money for time.

Busy parents, for instance, frequently go heavily into debt in an attempt to compensate for guilt feelings associated with not being able to spend as much time with their children. In many cases, both the parents and the children come to believe that money and things are the equivalent of love. Unfortunately, this kind of situation is likely to become more prevalent in today's world of dual-income families, reconstituted families, and divorced or separated parents.

Marriage Esteem Needs: To reach this level, you need to have self-esteem and esteem of your spouse, mutual respect, honoring of commitments.

In attempting to achieve sufficiency at Level 4, individuals must consider both the need for self-esteem and the need for spouse esteem. A person will most likely satisfy self-esteem needs through developing his or her full potential. By developing individual talents, a person becomes more capable of making contributions and therefore is more likely to achieve a sense of significance and relevance; as a consequence, such a person is more likely to experience a sense of self-worth and self-respect. Spouse esteem, on the other hand, usually comes when a person's contributions are recognized and appreciated by his or her partner.

Crucial to achieving sound financial practices, as well as a sense of personal fulfillment at this level, are the couple's intentions. Are their intentions to express their self-worth or to impress each other with how much they think they are worth? Self-worth is often expressed through what a spouse can or cannot do and at what skill level. In contrast, impressing one's spouse is often expressed through what he or she can and cannot buy and at what price.

Marriage Actualization Needs: Because the lower needs have been met, one or both spouses can support each other to reach respective goals, each can sacrifice their own needs (to a healthy degree) for the bigger picture, they have maturity, they maintain a healthy balance in life, each feels a sense of fulfillment in life and they give back to the community.

As a self-actualizing couple, each spouse has grown to realize a great deal of his or her potential. Each will have achieved sufficiency in the levels of physiological needs, safety needs, love and belonging needs, and esteem needs. They are now better able to be for the sake of being and do for the sake of doing. For example, one spouse may choose to be a sculptor because he or she wants to be a sculptor—to sculpt for the sake of sculpting. Such a person does not work for the purpose of winning a prize or solely to earn money but rather to experience his or her creative abilities.

For couples who are self-actualizing, work is often perceived as a medium for self-expression. They may very well earn a living, but it is an inner satisfaction they seek rather than fame or fortune. However, the ability to earn a living through a form of self-expression is usually made possible only if they have truly satisfied their lower needs; otherwise, their work may still be dedicated to seeking tribute, recognition, or material gain.

Developing a means of self-expression is an expansion of efforts to maintain lower-need levels and not a substitute for these efforts. Self-actualizing people are often better able to recognize and accept the realities of life and the fact that they will not be able to be, do, or have everything. They therefore tend to be as efficient as possible with their time, energy, and money in order to achieve a balance in the allocation of their resources.

In contrast, some individuals remain preoccupied with thoughts of becoming rich and frequently indulge in daydreams about what life would be like if they were wealthy. As a consequence, their expectations of how much money they will make, as well as how quickly they will make it, tend to be somewhat unrealistic. Such individuals tend to spend money they don't have and as a consequence often incur large debts. However, rather than facing up to the reality of the situation, they frequently develop elaborate, and often complicated, manipulative techniques to maintain the appearance of being able to live at a given economic level.

Self-actualizing people are not "super-persons" but rather individuals capable of responsibly expressing their individuality as fully as possible. Self-actualizing individuals are not likely to attempt to be someone they are not, nor to live in the past or too far in the future. Their budgets tend to reflect these values. Credit is used sparingly so as to avoid an over commitment of today's labors to the payment of a debt resulting from yesterday's consumption. Rather than comparing themselves to others and spending competitively, self-actualizing couples tend to concentrate more on self-improvement and devote their monies toward this end. Rather than being overly involved with wishful thinking and fantasy, which often lead to the development of unrealistic expectations and unfulfilling life-styles, self-actualizing individuals tend to organize financial goals so that whatever is necessary and sufficient has first priority.

We have all been taught that, when it comes to marriage, "love is all you need" and, as a society, we often focus on maintaining this love. But what we are not taught is that we must feed, water and nurture our marriage by meeting the lower needs of the union.

When we as humans don't have our basic needs met, we become more pushy, aggressive and fear-based. When we feel safe, comfortable, loved and esteemed, we tend to have more confidence, ease and trust that we will continue to get what we need.

What's Next?

There is no doubt that the 20th century has been one of change and in many ways, one of progress. As to how much the American family has progressed or benefited from this change is a matter of great debate. At the turn of the century, in a primarily agricultural society, the needs of the family came first in deference to the needs of the individual. As we prepare to enter the 21st century, the needs of the individual appear to come first in deference to the needs of the family. An individual's worth used to be measured more by what he or she could contribute, whereas in today's world, an evaluation of individual worth appears to depend more on what he or she can consume. During the 20th century, we may have become a society that loves things more than people, and as a consequence, many have come to believe that relationships are undependable and that all we have to do is acquire more things in order to be happy. As a counter perspective to such a belief, I proposes that we all contemplate the adage "You can never get enough of what you don't need because what you don't need can never satisfy you" (Poduska, in press).

The changing of society has also altered the family dynamic tremulously. Since both members of the married couple are working full time and often the same hours, the household chores and many other tasks have deviated from the traditional "his duties and her duties". This change has created conflict and disagreements. "Who does the household chores"? This topic will be discussed in the Common Sense Chapter.

Chapter 2

Communication

In marriage the word communication is perhaps the most often used word during any counseling session. I have counsel with countless married couples and I feel safe to say that 98 percent of them mention the phrase, *"we cannot communicate"* or the other part of that **he or she will not listen to me**. On one of my assessment tools I have each member of the marriage to list the top five reasons he or she feel is the cause of their troubled relationship. The word Communication shows up in the five assessment areas of each member and very often at the top of the list. Why is there a perception that communication is the primary cause of marital relation problems?

The problem with the perception that we do not communicate; is we always communicate something even when we try not to. Being silent communicates something to the receiver. The problem lies in *"what and/or how we communicate"*. Before we get into the causes or communication breakdown let's take a look at the mechanics of communication.

BASIC COMMUNICATION PROCESSING MODEL
Figure 1

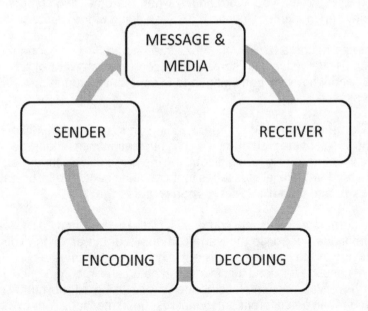

There is always a sender and a receiver in communication. At least there is an intended receiver. The model above depicts the basic processing of a message. Each message must have a **Sender** to direct a **Message** through some type of media (word, sound, written, texting, facebooking, twitting or though other high-tech and social media means). There must be a **Receiver** who will decode and interpret then feed it back to the sender. The sender will encode and determine if the message received match the intended message.

According to many experts there are three core areas of communication; The Communication Components, The Communication Message, and The Communication Process. Let's look and explore the three major areas in communication:

The Communication Components: The components of communication divergence into 3 arguments, they are **words**, **tone** and **non-verbal,** (normally referred to as body language). All three components take up a certain percentage of the message meaning.

Words equate to approx. 7% of the message, **tone** 35% and Non-**verbal** 58%. I think this may differ depending on the context of the communication, but the interesting point here is how little words contribute in the overall percentage amount. How much time do you spend trying to get your words right, when the other two components far outweigh in their contribution to the meaning of the message.

According to some experts the next time you are in an important face to face conversation with someone, become more aware of how you sound and what your body language is contributing to the meaning of the message.

The Communication Message: Leading on from the components we can now look at the next area, the communication message. When you are conducting face to face dialogue the message can be separated into 2 independent parallel messages that are being sent. The **information message** and the **emotional response message**.

The information message comprises of the words and facts, whilst the emotional response message comprises of the emotions you are conveying in the message. This explains why sometimes a communication message can lead to misunderstanding and in-congruence. How often have you spoken to someone who is using all the right words but you receive a different emotional response message. For example you may have experienced this common thought *"What they're saying sounds fine but I don't know what it is. I just don't trust them."* Another example may be when someone is telling you what they perceive you want to hear, but at the emotional level you just don't feel comfortable with the emotional responses you are receiving. Something doesn't fit.

Most people have not been taught how to communicate about some of the underlying feelings they are experiencing. This would explain why people focus more on the information portion of the message because it seems easier. Part of this is probably cultural conditioning; the other part is most people have never learned how.

Next time you are in a conversation, become more aware of what feelings you are experiencing during the communication. If you start to feel uncomfortable or not sure, just slow the communication down and ask more questions to help clarify what is really being said. Don't just rely on their information message for the meaning.

The Communication Process: The third core area of communication relates to the systematic way communication works. Simply explained there are 3 steps. 1. Producing and sending the message, 2. Receiving and interpreting the message 3. The giving and receiving of feedback. Most people do this by second nature so the suggestion is to become more strategic and aware of using the 3rd point of feedback. Use more questioning techniques to help drill down in order to gain the correct interpretation.

In Summary—In order to tie all three points into something practical this is what I suggest. Next time you are having face to face communication with someone, focus on becoming more reflective in your style by asking more questions or paraphrasing to gain clarity. Doing more of this helps to slow down the communication to give you more time to identify some of the drivers that may be forming in-congruent emotional response messages, as well as checking the non-verbal expressions that they are sending.

The Sender and Receiver have different perceptions. They each have their own worldview formed by their experiences, their perceptions, their ideas, etc. They will perceive, experience, and interpret things differently. The same event will always be perceived a little different by each of two people.

For effective communication to appear there must be some kind of common views. The participants must have some kind of concept of each other's location and of a possible channel of communication existing between them. They must agree sufficiently on these common views to assure that communication is taking place.

To have effective communication one needs to take all the factors into consideration. The different perceptions, the space the communication takes place in, verbal as well as non-verbal messages, the intended meaning versus the perceived meaning and the three major areas of the communication message.

THE MESSAGE HIERARCHY
Figure 2

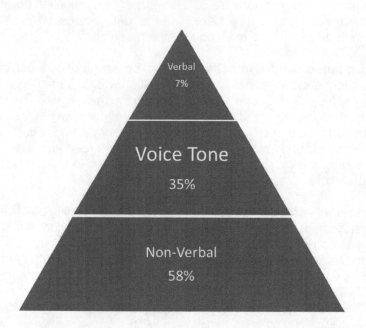

Words equate to approx. 7% of the message, **tone** 35% and Non-**verbal** 58%. This may differ depending on the context of the communication, but the interesting point here is how little words contribute in the overall percentage amount. How much time do you spend trying to get your words right, when the other two components far outweigh in their contribution to the meaning of the message.

Communication Breakdown

The effects of poor communication on a relationship can threaten the existence of the relationship itself. The symptoms of communication breakdown include feeling like the other person is not listening, arguing constantly, feeling like nothing of substance is being said and defensiveness, among many other warning signs. All of these symptoms of communication breakdown serve to create an obstacle toward problem resolution.

After communication breakdown has set into a relationship, if the situation is not quickly resolved through open and positive communication, more problems begin to set in. The opportunity that poor communication creates for problems to enter the relationship intensifies with each instance of poor communication. Poor communication makes it difficult for couples to relate to each other. Without the ability to relate to each other, the parties may begin to second-guess the relationship itself. Poor communication skills often lead to misunderstandings, which only lead to further problems.

In reality, 80 percent of communication that is interpreted is of the nonverbal sort, such as body language and facial expressions. In a relationship in which poor communication is common, relationship burnout is common. Burnout in this case means that the relationship stops functioning on an emotional level and the two parties begin to withhold information from each other. Betrayal often result, in the form of cheating or placing trust in other people. The further a relationship is allowed to deteriorate because of poor communication, the more difficult it is to regain trust and return the relationship to what it once was.

THE SPIRITUAL MODEL

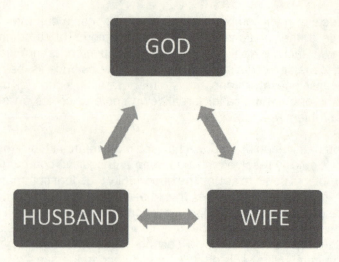

Communication in marriage ranks high among the primary causes of divorces. Although Infidelity and finances are ahead of communication according to stats, but in those two areas communication is often blamed for those causes as well. The spiritual model above represent a Christian Marriage that consist of three entities within the relationship; God, Husband and Wife.

This model suggests that when communication fails between husband and wife the communication lines are still connected via way of God. This means the spouses can still communicate to each other by going through God, even though the lines between the spouses are broken.

Non-Verbal part of the message is approximately 58 percent of the message, How Does It Affect the Relationships?

Non-verbal communication can tell your partner more about what you are thinking than your words.

Non-verbal communication can be deliberate or reactionary. It sends messages to your partner, and while it may never be verbalized, it is important for you to understand the meaning of the messages that you are sending your partner.

Harmful

Non-verbal communication can push partners away from each other due to hurtful feelings. These flashes of emotion are generally reactionary and occur before we give thought to their meaning. You can breach the distance with honest communication; however, hurt feelings can remain.

Misunderstood

Non-verbal communication can result from areas of stress outside of your relationship. Outside influences can be mistaken as relationship problems and lead to hurt feelings or distance between partners. Open discussion about outside problems prevent these misunderstandings from getting worse.

Is Communication Breakdown the Root Cause of Marriage Break-up?

This is what Kelvin Ken said in an article titled "**Communication Breakdown**. "Communication does not mean the giving of thoughts, messages or information or the receiving of thoughts, messages or information, *but*, the exchange of thoughts, messages or information. Breakdown of communication is one of the most common causes of divorce in marriages. The exchange of thoughts, messages and information is where most couples struggle. This happens to most of us. Even those believing themselves to be compatible still found themselves facing this communication breakdown problem when they least expect it. They think they know their partners well, but the truth is they do not and sometimes end up facing marriage break-up.

Learning to listen to your spouse may take effort and practice, but listening is something that you must do in order to have a good marriage and be able to resolve problems. If you are not listening when your spouse talks and I mean really listening, then you are probably frustrating your spouse and hurting your marriage.

You need to listen as well as talk in order to truly communicate. Do you take the time to talk to your spouse about things that are important to them? If your conversations consist of" Hi, how was your day . . . Fine, how was yours", you need to make an effort to sit down and really talk.

Make an effort to talk to your spouse and get to know them all over again.

Married couples should compromise with each other regardless of how big or small their flaws are. But of course it is much easier said than done.

Listening and talking, the two parts of a conversation, you need both in order to communicate with your spouse and avoid contributing to one of the common cause of divorces."

What does the Bible say about communication?

The Bible provides us with significant wisdom and guidelines in the way we communicate to each other. Listed below are some passages of scriptures that will aid and improve the communication breakdown.

Proverbs 10:19-21

> *"When words are many, sin is not absent, but he who holds his tongue is wise. The tongue of the righteous is choice silver, but the heart of the wicked is of little value. The lips of the righteous nourish many, but fools die for lack of judgment".*

Psalm 19:14

> *May the words of my mouth and the meditation of my heart be pleasing in your sight, O LORD, my Rock and my Redeemer.*

Ephesians 4:29-32

> *Do not let any unwholesome talk come out of your mouths, but only what is helpful for building others up according to their needs, that it may benefit those who listen. And do not grieve the Holy Spirit of God, with whom you were sealed for the day of redemption. Get rid of all bitterness, rage and anger, brawling and slander, along with every form of malice. Be kind and compassionate to one another, forgiving each other, just as in Christ God forgave you.*

Colossians 4:6

"Let your conversation be always full of grace, seasoned with salt, so that you may know how to answer everyone".

One of the most effect ways to improve communication in a married relation is through

Prayer: It is often said that our primary means of talking to God is **Prayer.** The Spiritual Model that is illustrated above is based on the communication between "God / Husband", "God /Wife", and "Husband/ Wife". The lines that lead to God are prayer lines whereas the communication lines between Husband and Wife could represents the components of the *message hierarchy (***Verbal, Non-Verbal or Voice Tone***)*. Let look at prayer as defined by the author.

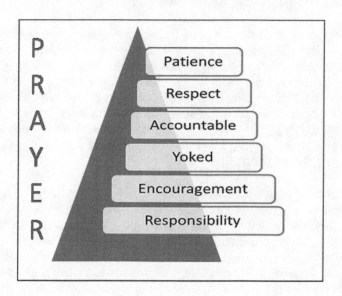

Patience

Learning the Importance of Patience According to the Bible

It seems as though in today's time that everyone seems to be in a heated rush, and our every movement is based upon how fast we can get from point A to Z. The world does seem to be a more hectic place, and in conclusion-we strike our own fate without even knowing it, or even still, not acknowledging time to take pause. We live in a world where the many tasks we face sometimes seem overwhelming; this is why it is of the highest priority to understand why patience is a virtue not to be taken lightly. And when the wind of change seems to overwhelm your life and it seems as though there is not enough time to accomplish your daily task, this verse from **Ecclesiastes 1:6** gives an in-depth emanating to the brevity of patience. "The wind goes toward the south, and turned about unto the north; it whirled about continually, and the wind returned again according to its circuits." The depth of this verse gives us a spiritual resource to draw from, not only does it mention about the brevity of time itself, it also encapsulates and illustrates on how we do not own time.

What does the Bible say about patience?"

When everything is going our way, patience is easy to demonstrate. The true test of patience comes when our rights are violated—when another car cuts us off in traffic; when we are treated unfairly; when our coworker derides our faith, again. Some people think they have a right to get upset in the face of irritations and trials. Impatience seems like a holy anger. The Bible, however, praises patience as a fruit of the Spirit (Galatians 5:22) which should be produced for all followers of Christ (1 Thessalonians 5:14). Patience reveals our faith in God's timing, omnipotence, and love.

Although most people consider patience to be a passive waiting or gentle tolerance, most of the Greek words translated "patience" in the New Testament is active, robust words. Consider, for example, Hebrews 12:1: "Therefore since we also are surrounded with so great a cloud of witnesses, let us lay aside every weight and the sin which so easily besets us, and let us run with patience the race that is set before us" (NKJV). Does one run a race by passively waiting for slow-pokes or gently tolerating cheaters? Certainly not! The word translated "patience" in this verse means "endurance." A Christian runs the race patiently by persevering through difficulties. In the Bible, patience is persevering towards a goal, enduring trials, or expectantly waiting for a promise to be fulfilled.

Everything that we set out to do on this earth is filled with labor, and this is why patience is a form of diligence when our life seems to be moving at the speed of light. This is why Christians should not get distressed with the complexities of the world at hand. **Ecclesiastes 1:6**, "all things are full of labour; man cannot utter it: the eye is not satisfied with seeing, nor the ear filled with hearing." Many people travel their life without ever truly learning the importance of patience; this can be said for many of the youth today.

Many of the youth today have no form of discipline in their homes, and in turn seek instant gratification and rewards without earning ownership of them. Learning to have patience in our lives teaches us to be better stewards in how we spend our time, and how we cope when things don't always go our way. **Ecclesiastes 2:14**, "I have seen all the works that are done under the sun; and, behold, all is vanity and vexation of spirit."

Learning to have patience also teaches us to have respect for our fellow man, providing us with insight to be kind to our elders, and in return we grow exponentially in our personal lives. **Proverbs 11:1**, "a false balance is abomination to the LORD: but a just weight is his delight." When we begin to balance our lives we also become a patient observer to what is important today and what can be resolved for another day. **Proverbs 15:14**, "The heart of him that hath understanding seeketh knowledge: but the mouth of fools feedeth on foolishness."

The next time you are in a traffic jam, betrayed by a friend, or mocked for your testimony, how will you respond? The natural response is impatience which leads to stress, anger, and frustration. Praise God that, as Christians, we are no longer in bondage to a "natural response" because we are new creations in Christ Himself **(2 Corinthians 5:17)**. Instead, we have the Lord's strength to respond with patience and in complete trust in the Father's power and purpose. "To those who by persistence in doing good seek glory, honor and immortality, he will give eternal life" **(Romans 2:7)**.

In a marriage relation, patience is one the essential Ingredient that influences a successful marriage. With patience we can better understand our spouse, we will have more success in resolving conflicting issues, and it allows time to roll back anger which aid in controlling what comes out of our mouth.

Respect

What does Respect Mean?

Respect has several meanings and mean different things to different people. Having respect for a person is treating them with the utmost kindness. Treat them as you want to be treated. At other times respect can just be a form of greeting or gesture.

Every human being of every nation, irrespective of their power or strength, has the right to be respected. "Respect is an unassuming resounding force, the stuff that equity and justice are made of. It means being treated with consideration and esteem and to be willing to treat people similarly. It means to have a regard for other peoples' feelings, listening to people and hearing them, i.e. giving them one's full attention. Even more importantly, respect means treating one with dignity. Respect is the opposite of humiliation and contempt. So where the latter can be a cause of conflict, the former and its opposite can help transform it. As *William Ury* writes in his book *The Third Side*: "Human beings have a host of emotional needs for love and recognition, for belonging and identity, for purpose and meaning to lives. If all these needs had to be subsumed in one word, it might be respect".

That's a deep question. Part of respect in your relationship is learning to treat the other person how they want and need to be treated instead of expecting them to settle for what you think you should do for them. Treating them like the most welcome and special guest in your life and using good manners around them. Take care of their feelings, their trust in you and their belongings as if they are the most special gifts that you have ever been given. That's the basics . . . .

You learn what is important to your mate. You have consideration for their wants and needs and respect their wishes. If they have a different religious belief than yours you learn to respect that just as they should respect yours. This goes with all facets of your married life. You don't purposely do something that you know your mate would object to, you respect their feelings.

Importance of Respect in marriage

Respect is the first positive step in building a relationship and relationships are central to conflict transformation. One does not have to like a person or understand his viewpoint to accord him respect.

Respect comes with the belief that a person or culture can have beliefs contradictory to ours and we should still honor them, as basic respect is a fundamental right of all human beings. In addition, goals and concessions become easier to attain when the element of respect is present As Bill Richardson, the US permanent representative to the UN put it. "You have to be a human being. You cannot be arrogant . . . . If you treat each individual with respect, each nation with dignity, you can get a lot further than trying to muscle them".

Respect is created in many ways.

1. It is created when people treat others as they want to be treated. This brings us to the famous quotation from the *Bible*. "Do unto others as you would others do unto you". This also brings the element of circularity to it. That is, things are connected and in relationship. So the growth of something, such as respect, often nourishes itself from its own process and dynamics. Be the first to accord respect, and with time, it will develop amongst all the conflicting parties.
2. Avoid insulting people or their culture; instead try to understand them. Many disastrous interactions are characterized by attitudes such as arrogance, disdain, fear of difference, etc. To avoid this, it helps to contact people who are familiar with the unfamiliar culture and can give the peace builder guidelines of how to best adapt to the culture.
3. Be courteous. Listen to what others have to say. Treat people fairly. All the basic elements "that we learned in Kindergarten" will go a long way to creating an atmosphere of trust and respect.
4. Apart from the above, when already involved in a conflict, 'separating the people from the problem also allows one to treat the other side with honor. Recognizing that the issue is the problem at hand and not the people can also help create respect.

In summary both husband and wife has a great need to be respected and when this need is not met trouble in the relationship is Unavoidable. When a wife respects, nurtures, and affirms her husband, it deepens her love for him. On the other hand, when we don't regard something as valuable and neglect it, our feelings for it begin to wane. At the top of any man's list of needs is respect from his mate; God created men that way. He needs respect as much from his wife as he needs air to breathe.

A man who doesn't receive respect from his wife is a man who begins to wither on the inside. He's all right as long as no one is standing on the air hose running to the tank labeled Respect.

Men need to <u>love</u> their wives and not being harsh with them is showing them love. Love is a verb—it's an action, it's what you do. Saying I love you is important, but showing it by loving kindness, consideration, and a soft spoken tone is more important. You can scream "I love you!" but a tender, soft kiss tells your wife more than a hundred "I love you ever could. Women love to communicate while men are often silent, but when husbands take the time to listen, it births a godly love. Our actions can show love and our tone of voice can show consideration, but talking with your wife and *listening* is perhaps one of the greatest things a husband can do. And *not* while watching TV. Give your wife your undivided attention, make eye contact, and just sit and listen to her—let her talk. She doesn't need you to interrupt to try and fix things (men tend to be problem solvers); she just needs you to listen to her quietly. This tells her you value her opinion and that it's important to you. This shows the wife that you love her.

Accountable

Many people wonder what the Bible has to say about accountability. While the word "accountability" does not appear in the Bible, the word "accountable" does. The Bible states that leaders are accountable for leading God's people in the right direction. They are accountable for warning others when they are going the wrong way. God will hold teachers accountable for leading His people astray.

The Meaning of Accountability

By accountability, we are not talking about coercive tactics, the invasion of privacy, or bringing others under the weight of someone's taboos or legalism or manipulative or dominating tactics. Rather, by accountability we mean developing relationships with other Christians that help to promote spiritual reality, honesty, obedience to God, and genuine evaluations of one's walk and relationship with God and with others. We are talking about relationships that help believers change by the Spirit of God and the truth of the Word of God through inward spiritual conviction and faith.

Being what we are, sheep that are prone to wander, accountability to others is simply one of the ways God holds us accountable to Him. Left to ourselves, there is the great temptation to do mainly what we want rather than what God wants and what is best for others. So what is meant by accountability? We are talking about teaching, exhorting, supporting, and encouraging one another in such a way that it promotes accountability to Christ and to others in the body of Christ, but never by manipulation or domination.

Accountability is necessary because like sheep we tend to go our own way. We are all self-willed. We want to protect our comfort zones and avoid having to deal with certain issues that are important to becoming obedient Christians, which is one of the goals of the Great Commission (Matt. 28:19-20). Making disciples means teaching others to obey the Lord and this is very difficult without some measure of accountability. Accountability is part of the means God uses, as will be demonstrated below.

Yoked

Literally, a "yoke" is a device laid across the necks of draft animals to harness them together so they can work as a team, and their load is attached to it. Its use gave rise to a couple of figurative meanings in the New Testament.

If a yoke wasn't properly attached to the animals, or if the load was too heavy for them to pull, the yoke would chafe the animals painfully and hinder their productivity. Jesus made use of this bit of common knowledge among His audience when He taught, "*My* **yoke** *is easy and My burden is light*" (**Matthew 11:30**), wherein He was contrasting the "difficulties" of following Him with the difficulties of keeping the Law of Moses. (*"Now therefore, why do you test God by putting a* **yoke** *on the neck of the disciples which neither our fathers nor we were able to bear?"*—The Apostle Peter, speaking in **Acts 15:10**.)

The other major figurative meaning refers to the way a yoke places animals *side-by-side*, so they must both *match* and *move together* in order to accomplish anything. This aspect gives rise to the teaching, "*Do not be unequally* **yoked** *together with unbelievers.*" (**2 Corinthians 6:14**). This teaching is not exclusive to marriage; in fact, Paul wasn't even talking about marriage in that passage. It more broadly applies to **any** relationship that would compel two people to "work together as one."

Yoke in the case of this writer is use as a symbol of teamwork (working together to ensure the success of the marriage).

Working Together as a Team

"Working together as a team"—we know we've talked a lot about this on different levels in past marriage messages, but SURPRISE, we aren't done! And we never will be, because we so deeply believe that married couples are supposed to work together as a team. We believe this is part of "Cleaving" together in marriage (biblically-speaking).

One of the many areas of marriage in which we should work together as a team is in the area of doing work around the house. Yeah, we know that can be a dirty word in many ways, but it's a necessary subject to talk about because it leads to so many arguments. It's actually among the top 5 things that married couples reportedly argue about.

We know that in different cultures and parts of the world, it's "assumed" that the wife is supposed to take care of that aspect of living together. But our world is changing. Husbands and wives are taking on different responsibilities (such as both working outside of the home) in our modern world and so housework is becoming more of a problem.

Encouragement

"Why is encouragement so important according to the Bible?"

"But encourage one another daily, as long as it is called Today, so that none of you may be hardened by sin's deceitfulness," Hebrews 3:13 tells us. First Thessalonians 5:11 says, "Therefore encourage one another and build each other up, just as in fact you are doing." Throughout Scripture we see instructions to encourage one another and verses that are meant to encourage us. Why is encouragement emphasized in Scripture? Primarily, because encouragement is necessary to our walk of faith.

Jesus told His followers, "In this world you will have trouble. But take heart! I have overcome the world" (John 16:33b). Jesus did not shy from telling His followers about the troubles they would face. In fact, He told them the world would hate them (John 15:18-21; see also Matthew 10:22-23 and 2 Corinthians 2:15-16). But Jesus' grim forecast was tempered with cheer; He followed His prediction of trouble with a sparkling word of encouragement: He has overcome the world. Jesus is greater than any trouble we face.

Without encouragement, hardship becomes meaningless, and our will to go on wanes. The prophet Elijah struggled with discouragement (1 Kings 19:3-10), and so do we. It is important to remember that "our struggle is not against flesh and blood, but against . . . the powers of this dark world and against the spiritual forces of evil in the heavenly realms" (Ephesians 6:12). This truth makes encouragement all the more important. It is not just that we face the world's displeasure; we are caught in the crosshairs of a spiritual battle. When we are encouraged in Christ, we have strength to put on our spiritual armor and remain steadfast (see Ephesians 6:10-18).

Responsibility

We have heard of many people who jump into marriage quickly without fully understanding and realizing the seriousness of this way of life. Feeling so much in love, many young couples stop there and say "Nothing else matters as long as we are together." Does this sound familiar?

The next thing we know, some of them have separated. Why? Didn't they just say "as long as we're together?" From this statement alone, it seemed that both have not been properly informed and counseled on what marriage is all about, or their roles as husband and wife. When the honeymoon is over, reality sets in.

Marriage is not a game or a playhouse. It is the union of husband and wife. Through their love for one another, they have taken the step to live their lives together forming a family. Therefore an important aspect that a couple must take in marriage is responsibility. Marriage means responsibility.

I have met wives who are separated and who said that their marriage failed because her husband was irresponsible. We asked them in what way were they irresponsible? One response is that the husband just delegates his responsibilities to his wife. For example, he lets the wife work and take care of the finances while he just stays comfortably at home. Another said that the husband would run away from problems instead of facing them and finding solutions. Another one cannot handle the responsibility of taking care of children.

This happens vice versa when the wife too does not live up to her role as a wife and mother.

Haven't you heard parents say to their children "You must be responsible in doing your homework" meaning," it is your duty." In a similar way, husbands and wives expect the other to be responsible as a spouse and parent. When this does not happen, problems start to occur between them. We will start to hear the words "How irresponsible can you get!" "You should have done this or that!" Each one will start to blame the other.

Where there is love, one only thinks of the other spouse, therefore takes full responsibility to make his/her marriage work. Because of love, both husband and wife will then understand their respective roles and help each other concretize it. Marriage means responsibility.

Love does not delegate everything to the other but there is reciprocity between the spouses. Love even extends one's responsibility outward. It extends a helping hand. Love makes one accountable to the other. Love not only makes them responsible spouses but even makes them responsible parents.

Chapter 3

Functional Needs

As difficult as marriage can be to achieve, it is not complicated. And so, if I can't describe it in a page or two, then I've probably made it too complex. The true measure of a successful marriage is that it accomplishes the results that it sets out to achieve. To do that on a consistent, ongoing basis, a married couple must meet the five functional needs that are essential to a successful marriage. I am a great fan and follower of 'Patrick Lencioni" in is his book on the "Five Dysfunctions of a Team which align with my hierarchy of functional needs. I borrowed his model to further explain my functional of needs model.

Δ **Need # I: Trust:** In a great marriage couples trust one another on a fundamental, emotional level, and they are comfortable being vulnerable with each other about their weaknesses, mistakes, fears, and behaviors. They get to a point where they can be completely open with one another, without filters.

Δ **Need #2: Dealing with Conflict:** couples that trust one another are not afraid to engage in passionate dialogue around issues and decisions that are keys to the marriages success. They do not hesitate to disagree with, challenge, and question one another, all in the spirit of finding the best answers, discovering the truth, and making great decisions.

Δ **Need #3: Commitment** . . . couples that engage in unfiltered conflict is able to achieve genuine buy-in around important decisions, even when one member initially disagrees. That's because they ensure that all opinions and ideas are put on the table and considered, giving confidence to both members that no stone has been left unturned.

Δ **Need #4: Accountability:** . . . couples that commit to decisions and standards of performance do not hesitate to hold one another accountable for adhering to those decisions and standards. What is more, they don't rely on either member as the primary source of accountability, but both members are responsible.

Δ **Need #5: Respect:** . . . couples that trust one another, engage in conflict, commit to decisions, and hold one another accountable are very likely to set aside their individual needs and agendas and focus almost exclusively on what is best for the relationship. They do not give in to the temptation to place their needs, career aspirations, or ego-driven status ahead of the collective results that define successful marriage. Even when ideas or desires do not agree they always respect the other person's input.

MARRIED COUPLES HIERARCHY OF FUNCTIONAL NEEDS MODEL
Figure 4

Trust—is probably the most important ingredient in building an intimate relationship between husband and wife. Trust is something that can be cultivated and nurtured if you will follow the guidelines below.

The essence of building trust can be summed in one idea: Create a safe emotional space for your spouse. If you are not actively working to build a safe emotional space, then you are probably building an unsafe one.

Some experts define an abusive relationship in the following way. They suggest that an abusive relationship is one in which one person is afraid to express his or her feelings and opinions.

Needless to say, an abusive relationship is one where there is no trust. The key to avoiding abuse and promoting trust is to consciously strive every day to build a safe congenial environment. And let me say at the outset that, if you feel you are in an abusive relationship based on the definition I just gave, seek help immediately. Never tolerate abuse!

When infidelity, lies or broken promises invade a marriage, the trust between husband and wife is severely damaged. However, this doesn't mean that the marital relationship cannot be saved or available for close relationships with others of the opposite sex, or not spending the entire weekend at the golf course.

There is a third aspect of commitment, which Scott Stanley, in his book "The Heart of Commitment", refers to as "met-commitment". He describes this as commitment to being committed, or more simply, as believing in doing what you say you will do. It seems to me that this is the appropriate response to God, given his consistency throughout history in keeping his promises with the human race.

An article by Stuart Wolpert had this to say about commitment:

"What does being committed to your marriage really mean? UCLA psychologists answer this question in a new study based on their analysis of 172 married couples over the first 11 years of marriage.

"When people say, 'I'm committed to my relationship,' they can mean two things," said study co-author Benjamin Karney, a professor of psychology and co-director of the *Relationship Institute at UCLA*. "One thing they can mean is, 'I really like this relationship and want it to continue.' However, commitment is more than just that."

A deeper level of commitment, the psychologists report, is a much better predictor of lower divorce rates and fewer problems in marriage".

Accountability—The foundation of any relationship is trust. In a friendship, a family bond, a work relationship, and especially in a marriage, the other person should be able to rely on not just the truth of your words, but on the dependability, rightness, and consistency of your actions and your attitude. The basis of that trust is accountability.

In a healthy relationship, partners encourage, support, and help each other in a variety of ways. For example, my wife and I are both trying to move forward in our respective careers; we encourage each other and keep each other motivated. Accountability is just another facet of that.

Accountability isn't just a concern for recovering addicts. It is crucial in any relationship, and it applies to both partners. If either partner is acting in a way that is unhealthy for him or her, contrary to his or her stated goals or principles, or isn't in the best interests of the relationship, it is the other partner's responsibility to hold him or her accountable for that behavior.

It is important to remember that it is not your job to punish or judge your spouse, or to force him or her to stop or change the unhealthy behavior. You are *never* responsible for your partner's actions or decisions. Your role as a spouse is simply to point out, firmly but lovingly, that your partner is getting off track. What he or she does with that information is out of your hands.

Respect—Couples who make a habit of showing respect in marriage will likely avoid the divorce court. When husbands and wives strive to honor or present their mates in the best light possible, it goes a long way in building a happy marriage. Boosting a spouse's ego through admiration or public praise can actually be a deterrent to adultery or fornication. A man whose wife openly praises his ability to invest money wisely or succeed in business will be slow to seek attention and validation outside the marriage. Similarly, women married to doting husbands need not look for affirmation from other men. Reverencing and cherishing one's mate builds self-esteem and boosts confidence in a spouse who is not ashamed to exalt a husband or wife's virtues.

An escalating divorce rate among Christians and non-Christians may be evidence that showing respect in marriage has become a lost art. Nearly 50 percent of all first-time marriages end in divorce. One of the reasons for marital failure is alienation of affection sometimes caused by constant berating or faultfinding by a disgruntled spouse. Couples should understand that no one is perfect and humans are prone to make mistakes. A husband who has failed at numerous business ventures may still possess positive qualities or winning ways. A wife may be the worse cook in town, but have a personality that puts everyone at ease. The key to finding marital happiness is to overlook faults and focus on the positive traits a husband or wife possesses. Otherwise one or both parties will always be discontent in the marriage. Sooner or later eyes will begin to wander in search of that "perfect" potential mate, only to discover that there is no such animal.

Accepting positive and negative characteristics in a husband or wife makes showing respect in marriage easy. Wise men and women understand that in order to have the perfect mate, some imperfections may need to be remedied. You remedy character flaws, by helping to building positive character traits through encouragement or compliment.

Showing respect in marriage can help husbands and wives overcome negative traits. Instead of belittlement or faultfinding, partners can help mates become better. It won't be long until the list of negative characteristics fades from memory.

When husbands and wives focus on showing respect in marriage a defense is built against outside influences, especially the temptation to cheat. Unscrupulous or flirtatious men or women seeking to infiltrate a good marriage may not stand a chance in a relationship between two people who constantly build one another up. There are no loose ends, no lack of affection or admiration, and no open door to flattery from a strange woman or man. A man who is reverenced by a loving wife need look no further for affirmation. Similarly, a wife who is openly loved and praised by an admiring spouse need not fear losing him to another woman.

Chapter 4

Money Matters

Financial matter is among the leading causes of divorces especially in couples under seven years of marriage. In today's society many of the couples getting married are entering the relation as independent young adults who have accumulated personal properties, credit scores as well as debt. In most cases these issues are not reconciled prior to marriage. Trouble begins as infatuation wears off and realization sets in.

There are five concerns that this occurs:

1. Couples do not receive Pre-Marital Counseling.
2. Couples do not disclose their personal finance status including debts and credit rating.
3. Couples do not develop a financial plan with goals.
4. Without a financial plan, couples do not work from a budget.
5. When it comes to money matters, couples do not effectively communicate.

What is premarital counseling?

Article from Sexual Health by: Dr. Laura Berman

> "With divorce rates hovering at 50% in the United States, many couples are deciding to become better prepared for the reality and the challenges of marriage before taking the plunge. Pre-marital counseling is often a good first step. While there are many sources for marriage advice, pre-marital counseling on a case-by-case basis is more likely to be effective. Discerning issues of compatibility as well as values each person holds in high regard can be imperative for success.

The decision to walk down the aisle is not to be taken lightly, especially when one considers the daunting divorce rate. No matter how in love a couple might be, marriage can be difficult and overwhelming at times. It comes with amazing benefits, but it also asks a lot in return, such as honesty, commitment, openness, and communication. These are skills that take time and effort to hone and this is precisely where premarital counseling can be invaluable.

Premarital counseling comes in many different forms. Some couples attend required premarital counseling at their churches, congregations, or temples, while others seek out secular options. Some attend only a session or two before the big day, while other couples commit to a longer and more-involved process. To decide which is the best option for you, sit down with your partner and have an honest talk about what you both want out of the process.

Realize that premarital counseling isn't for couples who "need help" in general or for couples who aren't sure about their decision. Rather, it's for the forward-thinking, committed couple who wants to find ways to strengthen their bond and deepen their love.

Premarital counseling can help you work through all these feelings and discover healthier ways to communicate and express yourself.

Premarital counseling will arm you and your partner with the tools you will need to survive troubled waters in the future. No relationship is perfect and no marriage will ever be problem-free, but with premarital counseling you can learn how to survive difficulties with your love and your happiness intact.

Ultimately, you get from your marriage what you put into it, and premarital counseling can teach you how to put your best self forward and allow you to reap the amazing benefits of a happy, supportive marriage".

Part of the anxiety that couples feel regarding premarital counseling is a result of not knowing what they'll find when they walk through the doors. Here is what you can expect in your sessions:

Marital goals: Although you have likely dreamed about your future together, it's important to make sure that you actually sit down and talk about those dreams with each other. For example, what if you picture a houseful of kids in your future, while he wants only one . . . or maybe none? Or, maybe you envision yourself as a globe-trotting couple with a packed schedule, while he would prefer a homebody life.

It's important to talk about all your goals and hopes and find out what each of your expectations are. This includes not only your hopes as a couple, but also your individual dreams and plans. For example, maybe you dream of going back to school and getting your degree, or maybe you envision yourself quitting your job someday to pursue more creative goals. Will your partner be supportive and understanding of these desires? Does he even know of these long-term goals? Premarital counseling can be a safe, nonjudgmental place to bring up all these issues.

Disclosing Financial Status: The most common argument among couples are issues such as finances, and family drama among others. Therapy can help you to address these issues before they arise, whether it's setting out a financial plan (or maybe even a prenup) or discussing what religion you will raise your children in. Premarital counseling is all about working out these issues before they take on a life of their own and threaten your relationship.

Communicating Problems Related to Finances: What is the main issue in your relationship? Do you feel like he doesn't listen when you talk, or do you wish you could spend more time together? All these little problems are going to grow bigger and take on a life of their own if they go unresolved. Premarital counseling will help you head these issues off at the pass and treat the underlying problems (because when you fight about him leaving his dirty clothes on the floor, you are often fighting about some deeper, more personal problem, such as the fact that you feel unappreciated).

Many of the young couples that I've counseled flinched when the word "budget" was mention. I believe that they think you need to be a CPA or a mathematician to develop a budget. Budgeting is the process of planning how your income should be distributed to pay your expenses. If your income is less than your expenses, the budgeting process also involves assigning priorities to the expenses to determine which ones can be eliminated or reduced. A good budget also takes into consideration the payment of state and federal taxes, which sometimes can be reduced by taking advantage of government incentives.

Money is simple and consists of three basic elements: *Income, expense, and differences.*

1. **Income**—The flow of cash or cash-equivalents received from work (wage or salary), capital (interest or profit), or land (rent).

    Samples of income are as follows:

    - Wages
    - Social Security
    - Interest/Dividends

- Child support
- Alimony
- Pensions

2. **Expense**—Expenses are simply the events that result in money flowing out of the household.

Samples of expenses are as follows:

- Housing (mortgage, rent)
- Utilities (gas, electricity, water)
- Food (groceries, restaurants, carry out)
- Medical (doctors, dentists, prescriptions)
- Clothing
- Telephone (cell phone, Internet)
- Cable TV
- Credit card payments
- Transportation (car payments, bus, subway)
- Insurance (car, home, health)
- Taxes (federal, state, social security)
- Savings for retirement, education, travel, etc.
- Tithes (10 percent of your increase)

Differences (Variance)—The amount of money left over after expenses are deducted from your income. This variance can be positive or negative. For this writing a negative variance is referred to as "debt" and positive variance as "surplus".

Debt—is a true indicator that the expenses are greater than the income. If allow to continue will create a serious financial crisis that could lead to marital problems and since finances is among the leading causes of divorces It needs immediate attention. There are two options available; increase the income or reduce the expenses.

Surplus—is the idea outcome because growth and financial stability comes from the surplus. It's the surplus that allows you to invest, buy new cars, upgrade your home, and give to others.

Budget your income

Budgeting is the process of planning how your income should be distributed to pay your expenses. If your income is less than your expenses, the budgeting process also involves assigning priorities to the expenses to determine which ones can be eliminated or reduced. A good budget also takes into consideration the payment of state and federal taxes, which sometimes can be reduced by taking advantage of government incentives.

There are some important steps involving developing your budget:

- Identify your sources of income
- Identify your expenses
- Identify where your money is going (these are items other than identified on your expenses)
- Ensure the budget is realistic and the numbers are facture
- Select or develop a budgeting format. (many formats are online)

Increasing and getting the most from your Surplus:

Suggestion 1

Developing Emergency Fund (1 month Pay)

An emergency fund is for those unexpected events in life that you can't plan for: the loss of a job, an unexpected pregnancy, a faulty car transmission, and the list goes on and on. It's not a matter of *if* these events will happen; it's simply a matter of *when* they will happen.

Suggestion 2

Pay off all debt

List your debts, excluding the house, in order. The smallest balance should be your number one priority. Don't worry about interest rates unless two debts have similar payoffs. If that's the case, then list the higher interest rate debt first.

When you start knocking off the easier debts, you will see results and you will stay motivated to dump your debt.

Suggestion 3

3 to 6 months of expenses

Once you complete the first two suggestions, you will have to build your emergency fund to a more realistic amount. The one month emergency fund is to respond to small emergency, such as attending an emergency out of state, washing machine go out, car break down or assist family with an eminent situation. A minimum of 3-6 months of your expenses placed in the emergency funds or a special market account. Use this money for emergencies only: incidents that would have a major impact on you and your family.

Suggestion 4

Invest 15% of household income into Roth IRAs and pre-tax retirement

When you reach this step, you'll have no payments—except the house—and a fully funded emergency fund. Now it's time to get serious about building wealth.

Experts suggest investing 10%-15% of your household income into Roth IRAs and other pre-tax retirement plans.

Suggestion 5

College funding for children

If you have children now is the time to start a college funding investment. In order to have enough money saved for college, you need to have a goal. Determine how much per month you should be saving at 12% interest in order to have enough for college. If you save at 12% and inflation is at 4%, then you are moving ahead of inflation at a net of 8% per year!

The Magic of Compounding Interest

When you were a kid, perhaps one of your friends asked you the following trick question: "Would you rather have $10,000 per day for 30 days or a penny that doubled in value every day for 30 days?"

Today, we know to choose the doubling penny, because at the end of 30 days, we'd have about $5 million versus the $300,000 we'd have if we chose $10,000 per day.

Compound interest is often called the eighth wonder of the world, because it seems to possess magical powers, like turning a penny into $5 million. The great part about compound interest is that it applies to money, and it helps us to achieve our financial goals, such as becoming a millionaire, retiring comfortably, or being financially independent.

Albert Einstein called it "the greatest mathematical discovery of all time." For those who carry hefty debt on their monthly credit card bill, Einstein's law of financial physics is not good news. But for the savvy investor, the principles of compound interest can be used to make a substantial amount of money over time.

To tap into the money-making magic of compound interest, it's crucial to first understand what compound interest is and how it works.

Financially speaking, compounding is the exponential increase of an investment. But in simpler terms, compounding is interest you earn on interest.

For example, let's say you put $2,000 in the bank. If interest is paid 5% annually, the bank will give you about $100 in interest for the first year of your investment. If you leave that $100 in your account, it will start earning interest, too. The following year, your $2,100 principal balance will earn $105 in interest. Over time, this phenomenon turns into the powerful magic of compound interest.

Here are some important ways to make compound interest work to your advantage:

Use the power of time: Compound interest is most powerful over a long period of time. Looking at the above example, your $2,000 initial investment would double in about 14 years. If all the money remained untouched, it would earn twice as much interest between years 15 through 28. In year 29, you'd effectively be earning 20% interest on the original investment (sometimes called "yield on cost"), all without needing to lift a finger.

The earlier you start, the better: Whether you're in your mid-30s or mid-60s, it's never too late to start saving. If you can afford to put away even $100 a month, starting now, compound interest will duly reward you—even in today's low interest-rate environment.

For example, at age 33, a $100 per month ($1,200 annual) contribution at a 1.5% annual interest will turn into nearly $60,000 by age 70. If you start at age 66 this same investment amounts to just $5,000. Still, not bad. But, it clearly demonstrates that the longer you can let your investment sit and earn interest, the better.

Maximize your "compounding periods": The more frequently interest is paid, the more quickly wealth will build. Interest that compounds monthly will grow faster than interest that compounds quarterly or yearly. Therefore, to quickly obtain wealth, always chose the shortest compounding period you can.

Earn interest, don't pay it: Compound interest can work the other way, too. A typical credit card company charges 20% monthly interest on unpaid balances.

COMPOUND INTEREST SAMPLE CHART
Investment: $2,000.00 @ 5% for 30 Years

Year	Interest Earned on initial $2000 Investment	Total Interest Earned	Total Sum
1	$100.00	$100.00	$2,100.00
2	$105.00	$205.00	$2,205.00
3	$110.25	$315.25	$2,315.25
4	$115.76	$431.01	$2,431.01
5	$121.55	$552.56	$2,552.56
6	$127.63	$680.19	$2,680.19
7	$134.01	$814.20	$2,814.20

MARRIED COUPLES HIERARCHY OF NEEDS

8	$140.71	$954.91	$2,954.91
9	$147.75	$1,102.66	$3,102.66
10	$155.13	$1,257.79	$3,257.79
11	$162.89	$1,420.68	$3,420.68
12	$171.03	$1,592.71	$3,591.71
13	$179.59	$1,771.30	$3,771.30
14	$188.56	$1,959.26	$3,959.26
15	$197.99	$2,157.86	$4,157.86
16	$207.89	$2,365.75	$4,365.75
17	$218.29	$2,584.04	$4,584.04
18	$229.20	$2,813.24	$4,813.24
19	$240.66	$3,053.90	$5,053.90
20	$252.70	$3,306.60	$5,306.60
21	$265.33	$3,571.93	$5,571.93
22	$272.60	$3,850.52	$5,850.52
23	$292.53	$4,143.05	$6,143.05
24	$307.15	$4,450.20	$6,450.20
25	$322.51	$4,772.41	$6,772.41
26	$338.64	$5,111.35	$7,111.35
27	$355.57	$5,466.91	$7,466.91
28	$373.35	$5,840.26	$7,840.26
29	$392.01	$6,232.27	$8,232.27
30	$411.61	$6,643.85	$8,643.85

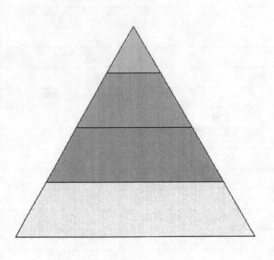

Chapter 5

Parenting

"Train a child in the way he should go, and when he is old he will not turn from it." [Proverbs 22:6]

"I believe that most professing Christians are acquainted with this text. The sound of it is probably very familiar to your ears, like an old tune. It is likely that you have heard it, or read it, talked of it, or quoted it, many times.

WHAT IS THE HIERARCHY OF NEEDS FOR A CHILD?
Figure 6

Children's hierarchy of needs

Understanding the basic needs of our children helps us as parents to meet our child's needs.

Abraham Maslow developed a useful model for understanding human needs. It applies to adults as well as children and is helpful to parents in prioritizing various needs and in understanding the ways in which we need to support children's development.

Maslow's theory holds true for children as well, however their needs different in process. For example they still need food, water, air, shelter warmth, and *Sleep* as their basic physical needs. When I talk about children needs figure 6 illustrates their needs slightly better than the typical pyramid.

Examining figure 6, we see that sleep is out front which further confirms its importance as a survival need. Why is sleep important?

Keep in mind that most children need lots of sleep. Often, says sleep expert Jodi Mindell, author of *"Sleeping Through the Night,"* if a child has poor sleep habits or refuses to go to bed before 11 at night, his parents will think that he just doesn't need a lot of sleep. That's probably not true—in fact; it's likely that such a child is actually sleep-deprived. To see whether your child falls into that camp, ask yourself these questions:

- Does your child fall asleep almost every time he's in a car?
- Do you have to wake your child almost every morning?
- Does your child seem cranky, irritable, or overtired during the day?
- On some nights, does your child seem to crash much earlier than his usual bedtime?

If you answered "yes" to any of these, your child may be getting less sleep than he or she needs. To change this pattern, you'll need to help him develop good sleep habits and set an appropriate bedtime. "Then they will get all the sleep he or she needs to be bright-eyed and bushy-tailed," Mindell says.

How much sleep does my child needs? Below are some general guidelines as to how many hours of sleep the average child requires at various ages. Of course, every child is different—some need up to two hours more or less sleep than others.

MARRIED COUPLES HIERARCHY OF NEEDS

Figure 7

Age	Nighttime Sleep	Daytime Sleep *	Total Sleep
1 month	8	8 (inconsistent)	16
3 months	10	5 (3)	15
6 months	11	3 1/4 (2)	14 1/4
9 months	11	3 (2)	14
12 months	11 1/4	2 1/2 (2)	13 3/4
18 months	11 1/4	2 1/4 (1)	13 1/2
2 years	11	2 (1)	13
3 years	10 1/2	1 1/2 (1)	12
*Note: number of naps in parentheses			

The other **physical needs** like food, water, shelter and warmth are as equally important. A child that is tired, hungry, or thirsted is not in a mood for playing or learning and they can't be expected to entertain themselves while you are doing something else until these basic needs are met.

Safety Needs—consisting of protection, security, order, law (rules), limits and stability will also vary from the needs of adults. All of those needs outlined in Maslow's theory apply to the children as well and since that information is address throughout the book, I want to concentrate on childhood safety. I asked the question online "what are the top five dangers that small children faces"? The results are astounding:

Top Five Deadly Dangers in Your Home

Parents watch out for their children and try to keep them out of harm's way, but many parents don't realize that the most dangerous situations for children often occur inside the home. If you want to keep your children safe, be sure to check your home for these common but dangerous situations that can be easily remedied.

Lead Paint

A surprising number of older homes still have lead paint in them. Young children in particular are prone to serious side effects from prolonged exposure to lead based paints. Toddlers may put old paint chips in their mouth, put their mouths on window sills or other areas where paint is peeling, exposing them to lead that can cause permanent neurological damage, headaches, behavioral problems, and eventual death.

If your home was built before 1978, it may have lead paint. Be sure the paint isn't peeling, flaking, or powdering into dust. If it is intact, your family will be safe, but if you plan on remodeling, you'll need to follow specific clean-up procedures in order to remove and properly dispose of the old paint. Don't ever try to remove lead based paint while your children are living in the house. Abatement specialists can help you minimize the effects of lead based paint in your home.

Unsecured Guns

Guns are dangerous in the wrong hands or untrained hands. There are several deaths every year that are the result of accidental shootings. The solution is obvious—lock up any guns in your house at all times. Your guns should only be brought out when you are actually going to use them (for hunting or target shooting, for instance).

When not in use, keep your guns out of the reach of children, preferably in locked gun safes. Be sure your children don't know the combination to your gun safe and that they won't touch any gun they may find in the home. Instead, they should immediately contact an adult.

Swimming Pools

Swimming pools are wonderful backyard additions, but they do mean potential risk for young children. In fact, many people pay higher homeowners' insurance if they have a swimming pool, which is sometimes referred to as an attractive nuisance.

Teaching your children to swim isn't enough. Even strong swimmers can drown if they slip and fall into a pool; an injury or simple shock can prevent them from saving themselves. Keep your pool surrounded by a high fence with a gate that is locked when the pool isn't in use. You may also want to invest in a pool alarm that will sound an alert any time someone falls into the pool so that you can quickly rescue anyone who has fallen in.

Medications

Chances are, you have several drugs in your home at any given time, but have no idea how dangerous the ones you have can be. Even over the counter aspirin or cold medicines are drugs that can be lethal in the wrong doses. Prescription medications are even more dangerous. A toddler only needs to take a few of some adult pills to have a deadly reaction. Keep your medicines out of children's' reach and be sure they are aware of the potential damage of taking someone else's medication.

Household Cleaners

Keeping a clean home is the key to keeping your family healthy, but many of the cleaners you use can also make you extremely ill or be fatal if swallowed. Some cleansers, such as ammonia, can also burn the skin or irritate the mucous membranes of the nose, throat and eyes when used improperly.

Clearly label all your cleaners, and then store them in a dry, safe location out of reach of children. Although it may be convenient, storing toxic cleansers under the kitchen sink is an invitation to disaster. Instead, label them as poisonous, put them on a shelf children can't reach, and properly dispose of all empty containers.

Your family can be safe and secure in your home if you follow our recommendations to minimize the impact of these deadly home dangers.

Safety is the need for freedom from anxiety and threat. It is hard to concentrate on anything when you don't feel safe. A child might need mom/dad to stay close in a new place until they feel safe and confident. When you are away from home participating in some social events and your child keep coming up to you pulling on your leg they are not being naughty or rude they just need to be reassured that they are safe.

In summary according to the federal government's statistics, fatal drowning remains the second-leading cause of unintentional injury-related death for children ages 1 to 14 years. For younger children between 1 and 4, the risk rises to make accidental drowning the biggest source of injury-related deaths.

For every one child who dies from drowning, another four children receive emergency department care for nonfatal submersion injuries

It is estimated that 890,000 children ages 1 to 5 have elevated blood lead levels high enough to affect intelligence, growth and development. Children ages 1 to 2 are at the greatest risk from lead poisoning.

Ingesting dust from deteriorating lead-based paint is the most common cause of lead poisoning among children.

Children are more likely to suffer elevated blood lead levels if they are low-income, receiving Medicaid, living in large metropolitan areas or living in older housing.

Each year, more than 20,000 children go to U.S. emergency rooms with gun injuries, a new study estimates. That number is 30 percent higher than what researchers had previously found.

Researchers at Children's Hospital Boston analyzed reports from the National Hospital Ambulatory Medical Care Survey of U.S. emergency department visits from 1999 to 2007. In those eight years, they counted nearly 186,000 children, from newborns to 19-year-olds, who had been treated for firearm injuries. About 8,300 of those injuries proved fatal.

The study found that non-Caucasian boys age 12 and older were most likely to be injured by a gun. Forty-seven percent of the injuries they counted were in the South, but the Midwestern states had the highest proportion of gun injuries relative to the population size.

Among children ages 5 and under, 60 percent of poisoning exposures are by non-pharmaceutical product such as cosmetics, cleaning substances, plants, foreign bodies and toys, pesticides, art supplies and alcohol; 40 percent are by pharmaceuticals.

Of the oral prescription drugs ingested by children ages 4 and under, 23 percent belong to someone who does not live with the child; 17 percent belong to a grandparent or great-grandparent.

When dispensing over-the-counter medications to their children, only 30 percent of caregivers are able to accurately measure a correct dosage.

A study in the September 2010 issue of *Pediatrics* (published online on August 2), examined cases in the National Electronic Injury Surveillance

System database of children treated for injuries related to a variety of cleaning products, including drain cleaners, ammonia, dishwasher detergents, swimming pool chemicals, laundry soap, bleach, toilet bowl products, abrasive cleaners, room deodorizers, and general-purpose cleaners. In 1990—the first year the study looked at—22,141 children age 5 and younger were treated for cleaning chemical injuries. By 2006, this number had decreased 46 percent to 11,964 injuries.

Safety needs is the second tier of Maslow's hierarchy of needs and for children it is essential that parents keep their environment safe and the children out of harm's way.

Belonging and Love Needs—are essential even though they are third on the hierarchy for the child's survival. Babies feed through their eyes and through their sense of touch as well as their mouth. Children need a sense of belonging to someone special, acceptance and understanding, affection, attention, affirmation and accountability.

Acceptance

Children will feel secure if their parents accept them unconditionally. They need parents to be non-judgmental and not compare them to others, accepting them as who they are despite their behavior.

Parents are advised to give their children positive reassurance and encouragement. Acceptance will help children to develop a sense of security.

For example, a parent should always remind their child that they love them and are special to them, just by being their son or daughter.

Affection

Parents need to show affection to their children. This is how their children know that their parent cares for them and loves them.

Parents can spend quality time with their children by talking, reading, writing, playing, massaging and hugging them.

When parents show affection to their children, their children will feel loved and contended.

Attention

Children love to have attention from parents. If the children have enough attention (quality time) with the adult, many behavioral problems and acting out may be reduced.

Sometimes, children misbehave to get attention from parents. Children prefer negative attention (e.g. scolding, punishment) rather than no attention (being neglected or ignored) at all.

It is advisable for parents to set aside some time to have some activities to communicate your love with your children.

A parents' availability gives importance and self-worth to children. When parents give undivided attention to their children, they will feel loved.

Affirmation

It is to give children unconditional positive feedback. Affirmation makes them feel importance. It helps the children to build self-confidence and self-esteem.

For instance, mother may say to her daughter, "I appreciate your attentiveness during the class. You are diligent. I am proud of you. It is my honor to be your mother."

Accountability

Children will feel-good that their parents trust them and count on them. They will learn how to take responsibility for their actions, how to make good choices about their behavior, and face outcomes from their choices. It helps to develop a sense of responsibility in children.

For example, a child spills his water on the floor. He asks his mother for a mop to clean up the floor. Mother says, "I recognize that you are responsible to clean up the mess.

By her showing her appreciation to her child's effort to clean up the mess, the child knew that he was responsible to face the consequences of his action.

When parents praise the character quality of their children, it helps them to develop good character and feel that they belong and are loved.

Esteem Needs—Children who are physically well cared for and feel secure and loved pretty soon are exploring their world, trying out what they can do and getting into everything. They cry 'look at me' as they show off some new skill, from the toddler who gets the wee in the potty to the adolescent showing off his computer skills. Success needs involve developing enough confidence in achievement to be willing to try new things, to have some self-respect and a degree of independence and freedom appropriate to the child's age. A two year old may put on his pants; a twelve year old may catch the bus to the movies with friends. If children are achieving at this age they are meeting the esteem needs.

Self-Actualization Needs—Maslow's term for the person who continually met their own basic needs and was not dependent on others' approval. Such a person is in "overflow" mode, they can focus on meeting the needs of others. Few of us are there for very long, life has a way of sending sleepless nights and bouts of the flu and overly busy days. Children are by nature dependent, and we can't expect them to be focused on others. As they grow they gradually get a sense that others have needs too. We teach them to wait their turn, to share, to think about what they are doing and whether they would like it if it was done to them. These things begin from about the age of three and develop slowly. It is wonderful when children give back to us, their love, smiles and gifts of kinder paintings, but we must remain responsible for being in charge as the adult. They cannot meet our needs and should not be expected to, although they can be taught to help.

Understanding the needs of your child is a major part of parenting. If these needs are not satisfied it impairs your child's growth and may prevent them from reaching the Self-Actualization level.

Another major aspect of parenting is discipline. Discipline of children contributes to a major cause of divorces. One may ask why disciplining of children play a role in divorce rates? On one of the research findings family problems was ranked as the number three causes, this what the report stated: (*3. Family Problems*

Family relationships with children, parents, in-laws, siblings and step-children are all sources of marital problems. Raising children increases stress in the home and can cause minor differences of opinion to become major rifts in a relationship. Discretion is the better part of valor when it comes to family and marriage.)

Why does discipline contribute to this family problem? Even though in marriage we become one in spirit, the fleshy body remains with each of us. That individual body was reared in a different environment and exposed to different parenting styles and that include discipline as well. In most instances the husband and wife style does not align. If this misalignment is not corrected conflict is foreseeable. If this conflict is not resolve divorce may be the end result. It is imperative that both parents are on the same end of the continuum so that the child cannot be in the middle and manipulate both parents.

Discipline

What is discipline? *Discipline* is the foundation for raising a child. Children thrive on structure. Providing proper discipline gives them the structure they crave, making it possible from them to act appropriately in any situation.

Discipline is the process of teaching your child what type of behavior is acceptable and what type is not acceptable. In other words, discipline teaches a child to follow rules. Discipline may involve both punishment, such as a time out, and, more importantly, rewards. It sounds so straightforward, yet every parent becomes frustrated at one time or another with issues surrounding children and discipline.

What style of discipline was you raised under? What style was your spouse raised under? As parents you need to identify your respective style. The most common styles are listed below.

Styles of Discipline

Authoritarian

Parents who employ the authoritarian style show a high degree of control and low warmth. These parents are strict disciplinarians with many rules. Misbehavior is often punished severely with yelling and spanking. While authoritarians reward their children for good behavior, they rarely show warmth and love. These parents believe that rules are necessary for children to remain under control, but children of authoritarians often develop a fear of their parents and may lie or become people-pleasers as a result.

Permissive

The permissive discipline style is the opposite of authoritarian, exhibiting low control and high warmth. Permissive parents worry little about control and give in to their children's demands. There is little structure and few rules in a permissive household, but the permissive parent sees this as loving. Outsiders will often view these children as spoiled, and kids of permissive parents often don't get along with other children because they are used to getting their way. In addition, children raised by a permissive parent can become insecure and lose respect for their parents.

Authoritative

While authoritarian and permissive styles do not teach children healthy ways to manage their emotions, authoritative parenting provides children with choices from which they can learn lessons. The authoritative approach, which is sometimes called democratic discipline, demonstrates high control and high warmth. It is a balance of the previous two styles in which parents set limits, offer emotional support and employ kind but firm discipline. Children are treated with respect and learn responsibility, but they also feel loved and safe.

Disengaged

A disengaged parent, called "neglectful" by some experts, does not provide structure or emotional support. The opposite of authoritative, disengaged parents show low control and low warmth. This parenting style exhibits low expectations and a lack of interest. Children raised by neglectful parents may be at high risk for emotional and behavioral problems, academic difficulties and low self-esteem.

Most parents exhibit all four styles but will have a dominating style that influence their way of discipline. A real problem will exist if one parent's style is *"Authoritarian"* and the other one's style is *"Permissive"*. The parents will always be in conflict or disagreement and the child will be confused.

It is very important that before a child enters the relation there are many conversations on discipline's styles. All differences should be worked out so that both parents are on the same page when disciplining is required.

Where significant disagreement occurs is in the area of sanctions. What are sanctions and what role do they play in discipline?

Sanctions are defined for the purpose of this book as methods used to change a child's unwanted behavior. Before I go too far, let's take a look at the Biblical view of discipline associated with correcting a child's unwanted behavior.

> "He who spares the rod hates his son. But he who loves him is careful to discipline him." (Proverbs 13:24)
>
> "Folly is bound up in the heart of a child, but the rod of discipline will drive it far from him." (Prov. 22:15)
>
> "Do not withhold discipline from a child; if you punish him with the rod, he will not die. Punish him with the rod and save his soul from death." (Prov. 23:13-14)
>
> "The rod of correction imparts wisdom, but a child left to itself disgraces his mother." (Prov. 29:15)

Many Christian couples ascribes to the biblical concepts of discipline specifically Proverbs 23:13-14 where it states *"Do not withhold discipline from a child; if you punish him with the rod, he will not die. Punish him with the rod and save his soul from death."* This is one area that Christians Couples must exercises extreme caution when they apply this sanction as a mean to correct unwanted behavior. Two particular reasons: Firstly, in many States it is against the law and secondly when inappropriately applied it could cause death to the child. View the National statistic on child abuse:

According to data from the National Child Abuse and Neglect Data System (NCANDS), 51 States reported a total of 1,537 fatalities. Based on these data, **a nationally estimated 1,560 children died from abuse and neglect in 2010.** This translates to a rate of 2.07 children per 100,000 children in the general population and an average of four children dying every day from abuse or neglect. NCANDS defines "child fatality" as the death of a child caused by an injury resulting from abuse or neglect or where abuse or neglect was a contributing factor.

There are many who will argue that whipping your child is not child abuse yet there are others who say that hitting your child is abuse regardless of the way you hit him or her. There is documented proof of harm done to children mentally because of corporal punishment (hitting).

According to Traic Pedersen *Associate News Editor,* Individuals who are physically punished are at greater risk of developing a mental disorder, such as anxiety, depression or another personality disorder, according to researchers at the University of Manitoba in Canada.

Approximately two to seven percent of mental disorders in the study were tied to physical punishment.

Lead study author Tracie Afifi, Ph.D., evaluated data from a government survey of 35,000 non-institutionalized adults in the United States, taken between 2004 and 2005. Almost 1,300 of the participants (all over the age of 20) had experienced some form of physical punishment throughout their childhood.

Many of these reported they had been pushed, slapped, grabbed, shoved or hit by their parents or adult living in the house. Six percent of these respondents said their punishment may have been more than just spanking either "sometimes," "fairly often" or "very often."

Individuals who suffered a harsh physical punishment were more likely to have a range of mood and personality disorders or abuse to drug and alcohol.

Almost 20 percent of those who remembered being physically punished had suffered depression, and 43 percent had abused alcohol at some point in their life. This is compared to 16 percent of people who were not hit or slapped who complained of having suffered depressed and 30 percent who abused alcohol.

Raising children is not easy. As parents who have raised children felt like we could explode if they did just one more unwanted thing. We wanted to react in that moment; using punishment as a way of making them behave. Punishment really says, "I am getting even".

The goal of discipline is to teach healthy behaviors in constructive ways. Children model what they see. When we are angry and take a time-out before correcting our children they learn self-discipline as well as imposed discipline.

As mention earlier sanctions are necessary in order deter unwanted behavior from your child. Sanctions are administer as punishment or discipline a more positive way of getting desired results. A quick look at *"punishment verse discipline": cited from the University of Nevada.*

Punishment:

- Means to cause pain
- Is used to hurt
- Creates fear
- Tears away at a child's self-worth
- Makes children feel unloved, small and powerless
- Offers no explanations or solutions
- Says that it is okay for people who love each other to hurt each other

Discipline:

- Means to help develop self-control and character
- Is used to help our children correct their unwanted behavior
- Creates courage
- Help a child feel loved, important and empowered
- Offers explanations and solutions
- Says that people who love each other do not hurt each other

MARRIED COUPLES HIERARCHY OF NEEDS

The parents are the ones who decide on when and how they want to raise their children and that includes discipline. The intent of the writer is to provide information and some guidelines to aid parents in making informed decisions.

Summarizes this session on discipline the writer describes discipline as follows:

D—Demonstrates acceptable behavior by example. Parents must model the correct behavior by their living.

I—Instruct and train the child in the way they should behave.

S—Support and protect your child so that he or she will feel save and loved.

C—Correct undesirable behavior with positive sanctions

I—Institute realistic rules and directives

P—Perceptive the ability to perceive or understand; keen in discernment of the child needs.

L—Love is one of the most important aspects of the discipline process. Love will make up for your shortcomings in other areas. You must demonstrate love by examples, such as the way you deal with anger, frustration, disappointments and with others who may have wronged you. Your love for the child should be unconditional with no requirements to earn it.

I—Insight is a clear or deep perception of a situation; a feeling of understanding; the clear (and often sudden) understanding of a complex situation; grasping the inner nature of things intuitively. This mean you need to understand the child's inner feelings as well as his or her desires and aspirations.

N—Nurturance generally means providing the basic necessities of life for children, but in a wider sense, it denotes general support, love, and cultivation for the growing child. In other words, nurturance is "parenting."

E—Encouragement . . . Children need a lot of support and encouragement. As they grow, they develop their own thoughts and opinions. It is important to remember that as a parent, you should encourage and promote this individuality, not squash it.

> *Children, obey your parents in the Lord, for this is right.* [2] *"Honor your father and mother" (this is the first commandment with a promise),* [3] *"that it may go well with you and that you may live long in the land."* [4] *Fathers, do not provoke your children to anger, but bring them up in the discipline and instruction of the Lord. (Ephesians 6:1-4)*

Parenting today is no easy task but it is an inherited responsibility. It comes with brining a child into the world. How you rear your child is a decision that parents make. Kids do not come with an instruction manual rather they come into the world screaming wondering what they did to deserve coming into this cold and strange world. The world they came from had heat, automatic feeding system and water as they needed it. Now that they are here and unable to care for their selves the parents become their lifeline.

> For I have chosen him, so that he will direct his children and his household after him to keep the way of the LORD by doing what is right and just, so that the LORD will bring about for Abraham what he has promised him." (Genesis 18:19 KJV)

> Train a child in the way he should go, and when he is old he will not turn from it. (Proverbs 22:6)

Parents remember the best way to teach your child is by examples. The way you treat each other, the way you resolve disagreements, the way you deal with disappointments, and the way you love the Lord.

Effective parenting refers to carrying out the responsibilities of raising and relating to children in such a manner that the child is well prepared to realize his or her full potential as a human being. It is a style of raising children that increases the chances of a child becoming the most capable person and adult he or she can be.

MARRIED COUPLES HIERARCHY OF NEEDS

Earlier in this chapter I mention that family relations including raising children, according to some researches is the number three cause of martial failure. Effective parenting will certainly aid in the reduction of failure where it relates to family issues.

Chapter 6

Common Sense Marriage

Most couples enter into marriage motivated, optimistic and with very high expectations. Then on honeymoon night the sparkles, lighted sky and flashing lights does not appear. What went wrong?

Marriage doesn't require special skills or best practice techniques to have a successful beginning. It does require that the relation is built on trust and strong physical and emotional bonds. Marriage can be as easy, or as difficult, as you make it. The key is to understand the simple and common sense of what makes a good marriage. I am not trying to minimize the complexity of marriage or indicate the simplicity of maintaining it.

Doris and I will be married 56 years as of February 2013. We entered marriage at a very young age and had no idea of what marriage was about. We had a physical attraction for each other and a unique passion. We were reared in two different environments with contrasting application of rules and standards. Because of the diversity in our upbringing it was more difficult in trying to establish common grounds in which to build a positive relationship. Admittedly there were many challenges in our way and either of us was prepared or knowledgeable of marital concepts.

What did we bring into the relationship? Well, I had observed my father and knew that I was responsible for housing, food, clothes, income and protection of the family. Doris was taught to cook, clean the house, washing and ironing the clothes as well as taking care of the children. These are just basic common sense things that were learned from our parents. How did those common sense things provide us with enough skillset and energy to be at the threshold of celebrating our 56th Wedding Anniversary? Reviewing Maslow's Hierarchy of Needs theory we were at the survival level and equipped to move to safety needs. The values we brought into the relation from our respective environments, along with the fact that I had an income, enabled us survive if we used common sense.

Here are 5 common-sense and simple points to engaging your spouse and enjoying a long-lasting and passionate relationship:

Talk: Communicate your need for intimacy, what you need to maintain a healthy level of physical intimacy and how to compromise so neither spouse feels like the burden of "giving" weighs heavily on one set of shoulders rather than two. If talking is to be effective there are some basic and common sense rules you need to follow:

1) Be honest and upfront with your spouse.
2) Be respectful to their ideas, perceptions, feelings and individual needs.
3) Be considerate and ready to compromise or sacrifice for the betterment of the relationship.
4) Never condemn or sabotage your spouse's suggestions, recommendations or statements.
5) Never try to resolve a disagreement while you are angry, frustrated, or emotionally upset.

Listen: Though it may seem rather obvious, often the first roadblock to marriage intimacy blindsides a healthy marriage because communication becomes one-sided. Communicating your physical needs accomplishes nothing if you are unable to meet your spouse halfway and place equal importance on listening to her or his physical needs. The importance of listening is this. When you are not listening you are not learning. When you are not listening you are preventing opportunities. The fact that you do not listen reveals the reality that your mind is closed. When you are not listening you are preventing intelligence. When you are not listening there is nothing new, there are only your reactions. If you wish to live life to its fullest, then listening is vital. There are some "common sense" rules when it comes to listening:

1) Be attentive to what your spouse is saying, make eye contact and be alert to your non-verbal communication. Give your undivided attention. Stop whatever you are doing, i.e. watching television, talking or texting on your cell or if you are in the process of doing something you cannot stop, ask your spouse for enough time to shut down.
2) While your spouse is talking do not interrupt. Allow him or her to complete their speaking. Seek understanding of what is being said by listening intensely.
3) Be non-judgmental. Always remember that your spouse's perception may not align with yours; which do not mean it is right or wrong.

Compromise/Collaboration: Disagreements in a married relation will occur unless the spouses are identical and we know that is unlikely. Disagreements often lead to conflict and conflict must be resolve.

MARRIED COUPLES HIERARCHY OF NEEDS

Collaborate or Compromise to Resolve Conflict—Compromise and collaboration are conflict resolution skills that help communication and relationships. Both compromise and collaboration are goal oriented strategies instead of personal agenda oriented tactics. Using these two strategies can resolve conflict and improve relationships. Allowing couples to move forward from conflicts and gain a better understanding of their relationship.

Learning to build practices of working with your spouse instead of against him or her in conflicts can revolutionize personal relationships. The stress of conflict with her/him can be reduced leading to more enjoyable interactions with each other'

Schedule Time: Busy work routines, family obligations and other distractions often mean marriage intimacy falls to the bottom of your priorities. Either you or your spouse make time for sex, whether it be at least once per week or whenever you can escape responsibilities and distractions, or you risk romance falling by the wayside.

Get Away: Sometimes stepping away from stress and obligations and enjoying a new adventure, a change of scenery and a break from the familiar can be the spark to put a fireless marriage back on track. Spouses need time to spend alone, away from family, work and the hustle and bustle of a busy world.

Many young couples who are just starting out often feels that they cannot afford to get away. Getting away does not mean taking a cruise, a trip to Disney World or going to Hawaii. A trip to the Local Park with a sack lunch and sitting on a stomp together has the same affect. How about a movie or a local play? I would suggest that couples set one day or night a week as a *date day.* Whatever day you choose, make it a priority and let only emergencies or urgent situations cause you to change it. Put great thought into the day that you select, allowing for arranging for childcare if necessary.

The five points above are just simple things we can do that require no great sacrifice on either spouse. Yet the results will go a long way in preserving and strengthen your marriage.

Who does the Household Chores?

Household chores have become major issues in today's marriages. In fact it has reached the divorce rate's top ten causes on various research polls. This lack of shared responsibility between couples really points directly to the husband. My take on this, the husbands are still operating under the old perceived principles "Her chores and My chores". This translates into she clean the house and he wash the car, cut the grass and other outdoors's chores. This was an excellent arrangement when the wife stayed at home. Nowadays both partners works and this arrangement is not practical.

This is what Michelle Aycock a licensed psychotherapist had to say about this new phenomenon.

"I am having problems getting my husband to help around the house. We have two kids, and I feel like I do all the housework, take care of our kids and work a full-time job. Whenever I try to talk to him, he just ignores me. How can I get him to listen to me and help around the house?

Unfortunately, this situation can be a major source of conflict with couples. I often hear from women that their husband or partner does not help around the house. You may feel as if you have another full-time job waiting for you at home. Working women do spend twice as much time as men on household chores and taking care of the children.

Before the children were born, the odds are that it was easier to keep the house clean. However, with children, there is more laundry to do, more meals to cook and more messes to clean. All the while you continue to beg your husband to do just one thing: take out the trash. One of the biggest mistakes women make is asking their partners for help with household chores. Asking for help tends to imply the chores are your responsibility to complete. However this couldn't be further from the truth. Chores should be a shared responsibility.

Being a couple is a partnership which includes not only sharing financial responsibilities, but also household chores and raising children. It is important for couples to set priorities that you both agree on and work toward. It will require both of you to do your fair share. Doing your part is a way to show respect not only for your partner but also for the relationship."

Husbands, you may not like what I am about to say, but the truth will set you free. "Husbands should not just share the household chores, also the cooking and kitchen duties". Most of us men can barbeque because traditionally that was a man's thing. However, we cannot eat barbeque every day or for every meal. Men, let learn how to cook casseroles, meatloaves, grilled chicken, pork chops, and all the other necessary dishes. One might ask where do I learn how to cook? Great question, your wife will be happy to teach you and while you are learning, why not make it an **Us' Time;** you may be surprised of the rewards that come from this effort.

A common sense approach is for partners to share this responsibility. They need to mutually develop a plan of how to satisfy these chore requirements in a way that is fair and reasonable. The plan should take into consideration work schedules and the person's ability to complete assigned chores. There still are some chores that are gender specific.

In my house Doris does most of the washing and ironing. The reasons are simple; I cannot iron very well and often put the wrong clothes together into the washer. Now on the other hand, Doris cannot mow the grass, wash the cars or paint the house so I do those things. Ironing, washing clothes or cars, and painting the house are not necessarily gender specific however it make sense for the one who is best suited for those chores be the primary implementer. It is vital that each spouse have the knowledge or skill to make certain the chores get accomplished if one of the partners is disabled. Common sense solutions are straightforward:

1) Take the clothes to the laundry
2) Call lawn services
3) Contact house painting contractors
4) Take the cars to a carwash

Marriage is a team game and spouses must work together as a team if it is to be successful. I asked Doris what was her take on marriage since she and I share the same marital relation. This is what she had to say:

A FEW COMMON SENSE TIPS FOR ENHANCING A MARRIAGE (Wife's Perspective)

As you have probably already read; Cecil and I were married at a very early age, at an age where the definition of love was thought to be hugs, kisses and holding hands. However, from the very beginning, and even with my limited understanding of what a marriage was really all about, there was a feeling between us that even until this day I am unable to describe. This feeling seemingly ignites when we are in the mere presence of each other. Contrary to what one might think, I knew from day one that I wanted to be married to Cecil forever and to spend the remainder of my life with him. Next to serving God, it has been my highest honor and greatest joy to have been Cecil's wife for fifty six years.

Listed below are a few tips important for a happy and lasting marriage

1. **BUILD A FRIENDSHIP:** Marriage built on friendship will definitely flourish. Friendship creates fun, makes communication easier, makes your tolerant level higher, and you'll never be lonely. There are a lot of factors that can rob us of our physical beauty, such as illness, disease and age. Aging is one entity in the process of life that is inevitable. However, if the foundation of your relationship is strong, Friendship is not affected by this. If you are truly interested in marriage for keeps and sharing a wonderful relationship with your mate, make sure you are his/her best friend. Don't forget that RESPECT is a mandate for friendship!

2. **WORK TOGETHER:** TEAMWORK! Life's constant challenges and demands require that married couples work as a team. Marriage is hard work, but couples must stand together. Practice at working as a team is essential to marital success. It is a given that team work is a crucial element in all facets of married life even when it is in some situations uncomfortable. Couples should especially remember to work as a team when dealing with finances. Money is one of the most common sources of conflict in marriage. Support your mate!

3. **EMPOWER YOUR MATE TO LOVE YOU:** The husband is the head of the marriage union. Empower your mate to love you by showing him /her that you appreciate him, that you want him to take care of you. Let him/her know that you trust their decision in making sure you are secure, safe and loved. I have let my husband know on many occasions that I want **him** to take care of me

totally. By the same token I expect him to want me to take care of him. Be willing to allow him to be the man. Let him know you respect and believe in him. Talk softly and kind to him/her.

4. **AFFIRMATION:** Pats on the back, a kiss on the cheek or mere thumbs-up are great ways to affirm your mate. According to experts every person has a need to be recognize or told; good job, I appreciate you, or you made my day.

"One definition of "to appreciate", according to the American Heritage Dictionary, means "to increase in value." If you have a vault of gold hidden in your house, to which you add a gold coin, a gold nugget, or a pile of gold dust each day, you add value to your wealth. Every time you open the vault door, you can measure with your eyes how big the pile has grown.

Appreciating a spouse has much greater dividends than hording gold in a safe. Each time you give your spouse a loving word of affirmation, you are heaping value on to him / her. He/she feels treasured and adored. But something even more amazing happens—when you verbally appreciate your spouse in all sincerity, his/her value goes up in your eyes, too. You see him /her the way you are describing him /her and he/she becomes more and more valuable to you. It is a win-win situation. With more words of affirmation, love grows."

Other ways to compound your love nuggets

What are Love Nuggets? This author defines Love Nuggets as those unscripted love acts you do for your spouse that are unconditionally performed.

- Just because greeting cards. You can lay it on his/her pillow, if he/or she work you can go by their office or shop and place a card in the car seat or tape it to their bathroom mirror. Be as creative as possible because the thought will earn the love nuggets.
- Men, opening the doors for your wife still works and that includes car doors, helping her put her coat on, gassing up or washing the car earn a few love nuggets as well.

- Occasionally, give your spouse a "just because" gift (does not need to be expensive) I suggest a collection piece if he/she have a collection. For example my wife collects *Just Right Shoes (the mini ceramic or glass shoes) so I try to keep track of what she have and I will surprise her occasionally with a collector's shoe. The results were compounded love nuggets.*
- *Even in this modern day where both spouse work full-time the wife in most instances cooks the breakfast. Husbands, allow your wife to stay in bed several times a month and you make and serve her breakfast in bed. If you cannot cook, no problem, just do cereal and coffee with a thank you note.*
- *Stay at home wives; greet your husband at the door fully dressed and with a loving smile. Always try to wear what he like seeing you in. Some husbands want their food right away so ensure you have food ready and the table set. I know some of you will say, my husband do not care about all of that. Believe me, they care and this gesture will earn you many love nuggets.*
- *Wives/husbands, remember to put on that favorite fragrance after your bath or shower and wait for that "umm you sure smell good comment". More compounded love interest in your bank.*
- *A mutual nice to do is whoever goes to bed first turns the bed covers back. I get a nice feeling when I turn the covers back for my husband. When he's getting in bed I hold the covers up for him to get under. He does likewise. Watch their smile! Just a nice to do nugget.*
- *Add value to your mate's day by seeing them off on their way in a loving matter. You'll be surprised how happy it makes your wife/husband feel when you walk him/her to the car, give a kiss and say "have a great day", or I'll be praying for you to day, maybe even have a blessed day.*
- *Bring a small treat occasionally. It's nice to bring a small favorite treat back from the grocers. For example, I know my husband likes Mountain Dew, so now and then I'll bring him one or a small bag or chips. We'll both appreciate this nugget!*
- *Husbands, all of us do not have two-car garages so one of the cars must set outside. If it your wife's car get up start it and allow it to warm up prior to her leaving for work.*
- *Wives, you know males have that little ego problem so acknowledge them when they complete the honey-do list or repair that leaking faucet even though later on you need to call the plumber.*

I understand that each marriage has its own DNA so couples will need to find out their respective DNA and what makes their spouse tick. It is imperative to know your mate, know what he or she likes and dislikes, and knows their favorite restaurant and meal. Giving your spouse love nuggets will greatly enhance and add value to your relationship.

Keeping the Flame Burning

The daily routine that gets inaugurated in a long-term relationship can be sedating to sexual desire. Work, commuting, and daily chores or other responsibilities can possess us; kids can be needy and demanding; and keeping a home, paying bills, preparing meals, doing laundry and hundreds of other tasks can absorb your energy very quickly and engender a feeling of being very tired, if not exhausted.

Couples that manage to keep the flame burning often have to work at it. It's not like when you were in your 20s and it was the only thing going. Often, adult sex requires conscious effort, romantic words and gestures, complimenting your partner on his/her "sexiness," affectionate touch, cuddling, seductive invitations, weekend romantic getaways and other activities that promote closeness.

Keep the flames burning by incorporating romantic and sexual effort into your relationship. Staying romantically engaged doesn't happen on its own it requires your intention, foresight, effort and persistence.

Keep your romance alive despite the chaos and craziness life can pose just from living in the midst of sheer reality. Resolve to offer romantic ideas for your spouse's pleasure, even if only occasionally, like cooking her favorite meal when you know she's had an impossible day or entice him into a bubble bath with you just for the fun of it. Little gestures like these from time-to-time can ensure that the flame you once had can and will burn forever.

Here are some additional suggestions on how to keep the flame burning.

- Make time for your love life—Do not let other priorities push it to last place, and don't wait until you're really tired.
- Wife, make sexual "dates—with your husband, and say "yes" when you are approached most of the time. Men who are

disallowed often stop trying, and are far more likely to wallop in anger and resentment.
- Entice your spouse—by leaving suggestive or seductive notes, voice mail messages, texts or e-mails telling him/her you think he/she is hot, sexy and attractive—and that you want him/her.
- Practice Two-Way Communication—many relationships fail because of misunderstandings. Effective communication skills are necessary if your relationship is going to survive. If there is a hint or vibe that your spouse is disconnected or you are unhappy about something, do not ignore those signals or feelings. Approach them and suggest an open discussion. You may be frustrated, angry or hurt and so may he or she, but always stay calm and reasonable. Your goal should be to resolve differences and the only viable way of doing so is through open and direct communication.
- Wife, communicate to your husband what he needs to do to help you get in the mood—be specific with him in explaining your needs and wants such as emotionally, verbally, affection, and what feels romantic.
- If you are hurt or angry with him/her, tell him why, and tell him/her what you need for that hurt or anger to lessen.
- Women, take the lead—Men love it when women initiate and act seductive.
- Look after yourself—spend time every day on your appearance and your physical wellbeing. Work out regularly, eat healthy and stay fit. Not only will your spouse like looking at you, but you'll feel better about yourself.
- Never stop courting one another—gifts, compliments and a loving embrace go a long way, especially when they are a surprise to your spouse.
- Etch out time to be together—sure, you're working, attending meetings, keeping the house, and helping the kids do their homework.
- Do unto others—don't judge too harshly. If you criticize, do so the same way you would want others to criticize you. Be kind and considerate.

When you think back to the days you and your spouse were dating, can you remember the things you said or did together that sticks out in your memory as something you will cherish for the rest of your life? Can you remember the days of holding hands; romantic candlelight dinners; talking quietly together while sitting by a roaring fire; picnics for two; walks in the park under the moonlight; laughing and joking about nothing in particular? How did it make you feel? Did you feel safe and secure, valued and appreciated? Truly loved? Can you remember the specific moment that you realized you had fallen in love with your now-husband or wife?

Those memories are the flames that hold your relationship together. Fight with every ounce of strength you have to keep them alive and burning.

Chapter 7

Marriage Preparation (Pre-Martial)

Marriage Preparedness

Research show that couples who are getting ready for marriage spend numerous hours and lots of money planning the wedding but very little time preparing and planning the marriage. From my perspective the priorities are reversed. Marriage is for a life time and the wedding is a one-time special event. Logically thinking will move one to conclude that the event with the longest expectation would require the most effort. It is the discrepancy between the two acts that inspired the writer to focus on premarital preparedness. Specific areas to be discussed are listed below:

- Pre-Marital Counseling
- Personality Assessment
- Childhood Environment
- Marriage Stages
- Gender Differences
- Financial Management Style

"Why is premarital counseling important?"

From a Christian Perspective—

Premarital counseling usually falls under the office of the pastor or leader of a local congregation. In some congregations, the pastor will not undertake to perform a marriage ceremony unless the engaged couple submits to a series of counseling sessions. Pastors are aware of the divorce rate, even in "Christian" marriages, and they are concerned that those they join in marriage have the best chance of remaining "married." They see premarital counseling as an important part of getting a young couple off on the right foot.

The Apostle Paul in his pastoral instructions to Titus tells him to equip others to teach the younger generation. This is counseling which has at its core the idea of teaching biblical truth, standards or absolutes in one's relationship to others. This is especially important in a premarital situation because we cannot use what we do not know, and adulthood is not a guarantee of maturity. It is therefore important that the couple who intend to form a union making them one in God's eyes be instructed in God's viewpoint concerning marriage.

Premarital counseling based upon sound biblical principles outlines the roles of the husband and wife as they relate to each other and to their prospective children. Pastoral counseling should be in addition to the nurturing and godly wisdom the couple has (hopefully) received from their own parents. Parents are responsible before God to prepare children for adulthood, and that includes marriage. Premarital counseling is an excellent way to clear the misconceptions about the roles we are to play in marriage and distinguish between God's standards and those of the world. Therefore, it is crucial that the pastor or elder doing the premarital counseling be doctrinally solid, secure in his own marriage and family relationships and in obedience to God's Word so that he is equipped to impart God's viewpoint clearly and without equivocation.

Solid, biblical premarital counseling may very well be the difference between a couple that seeks to put God's principles first in their marriage and a marriage based on human viewpoints and worldly standards that put relationships in jeopardy. Serious consideration on the part of the prospective bride and groom to commit to a time of spiritual premarital counseling—and their agreement to model their marriage after God's order—will bring clarity to how each views the other in their "oneness" in the eyes of God.

From a practical and Common Sense Perspective—

Premarital Counseling is a way for engaged couples to learn more about themselves, their partners, and their relationship before they are married. It usually consists of 5-8, 50 minute couples counseling sessions with a therapist. Many of these therapists use personality or temperament tests to help educate couples on how their personality works both together in harmony and against each other in conflict.

I know, most couples that are starry-eyed and in love don't have any desire to hear about each other's (or their own) faults. And yes, Premarital counseling can (and should) create anxiety in both partners. After all you're talking about spending the rest of your life with this person (and nobody is perfect).

But, the flip side to that is; through awareness of what you are both bringing into the marriage, you'll be better equipped to deal with the hard times when they come. Most marriages will go through hard times.

Premarital counseling process will allow you to gain insight about each of your expectations for the marriage, the issues that you have had since before you met each other, previously unknown concerns about your partner, and how all of these things interact/where you are likely to hit potholes together in the future. I can't express to you how beneficial it can be to have a jump start on your partnership in life and premarital counseling is a great way to do that!

Due to the brevity of most pre-marital counseling consist of approximately 400 minutes at the max. However, only the basic things are consider that most counselors' feel are essential. The following information will better equip couples to take on this challenge of marriage.

Personalities Are Different—

Excellent relationships take work. Accept the fact that relationships; whether they be marital, parental, companion or co-worker, are not easy to maintain. In fact, good relationships are hard to keep. However, we must never associate hard with bad. Wonderful relationships are worth fighting for.

Always, when I present the basics of personalities, people are curious about how personalities affect their relationships, usually with their spouse. They want to know if "opposites attract" and what that may mean for their marriage.

I am pleased to be able to share that my wife, Doris, and I have a tremendous marriage. While we certainly are not perfect people and we have our struggles, we agree that knowing personalities and understanding emotional needs gives us a distinctive perception on our relationship. We both have a powerful appreciation for the strengths we possess as individuals, which helps us truly love and respect one another. We are a team. I encourage any married person or anyone considering marriage to undergo a personality assessment. By knowing each others personality improves your understanding of the other spouse's behaviour their by enhancing communication, and reducing disagreements.

Personality models are often used to promote mutual understanding between couples. This understanding is aimed at improving interpersonal relationships, and promoting positive attitudes towards people who are different, such as **understanding, appreciation** and **respect**. They are not used to determine if a couple should marry or not marry, however, models can be useful in marriage by helping you to:

- Understand your partner better
- Appreciate your partners' differences and unique contribution to the marriage
- Recognize the reasons for conflict or difficulty, and enabling a two-way discussion of how such difficulties can be overcome
- Affirm the contribution of both parties to the marriage.
- Recognize your partner's needs out of the marriage, and enable you to structure your lifestyle so that the needs of both of you are met.

Personality Assessments may be obtained through most marriage counsellors and many acceptable assessment's tests are available online.

Does your childhood past influence your marriage relationship?

There is an adage; "you are the product of your environment". Does that saying have any merit? Yes, to a certain extent, we all are, but this doesn't mean we have to accept what we are given in life. We can change the way we are, if we create a new environment for ourselves. We all have free choice. Just because we we're born somewhere, doesn't mean we have to stay there. Just because our parents believe something, doesn't mean we have to believe it to. Just because we're told/taught something, doesn't mean it is true. We create our own paths in life. We can't change others, they have to do that themselves, but we can change ourselves.

The way we discipline our children, the way we manage our finances, our religious beliefs and the way we resolve conflict are greatly influence by our past and the way our parents executed those entities.

Research and studies indicate the experiences that married individuals had in their families of origin had a substantial impact on the quality of their marriages. Individuals in this study who experienced a stable, healthy family-life while growing up tended to have more success in dealing with the demands of their marriages and other intimate relationships. Those who experienced less functionality and more tension in their families of origin tended to have more difficulties in their marriages and intimate relationships.

There seems to be certain subjects that come up in seventy percent of the married couples I counsel; child discipline, finances and resolution of conflict. It was very clear that these subjects were approach differently by each member of the marriage and further study reveal that their respective view reflected their upbringing.

To answer the question; "Does your childhood past influence your marriage relationship"? Yes, to a certain extent, we all are influenced by our upbringing and childhood environment. In a marriage where a couple is striving to become one some changes are obligatory.

Too many couples deciding to get married do not understand the complexity of this union. The most common sense example I can marshal at this time is the coming together of two rivers to form one. In geography, a confluence is the meeting of two or more bodies of water. Known also as a conflux, it refers either to the point where a tributary joins a larger river, called the main stem, or where two streams meet to become the source of a river of a new name, such as Confluence of the Drava and Danuve Rivers near Osijek, Croatia.

This confluence was chosen because of the dissimilarity between the rivers. See picture below.

Drava and Danuve Rivers

The Drava River on the right has blue and clear water, whereas the Danuve River is dirty and mucked. Also you notice a little turbulence where the two collide this collision is liken to couples coming together and, a noticeable point as the rivers continue to flow they become one river with the composition of both. The lesson here, both partners bring composites from their past environment into the relationship and thanks to God we are blinded during most of the honeymoon stage thus giving us time to blend before the eyes open. This may be the appropriate time to identify the marriage stages.

Stages Of Marriage

Marriage can be understood better if seen as a series of phases a couple goes through their shared partnership. These seven phases are interrelated, but each is different and the way they separate from the others.

With this description of the phases of marriage, we hope to help you understand why certain things are happening, how to get a clearer view of your relationship and its possible future development.

Honeymoon Stage

The honeymoon phase occurs immediately after the wedding and continues from several months to a year or two. This stage is characterized by passion and intimacy, this phase is very important because it nourishes the union between partners. It is often said that the couple are wearing blinders.

Eye Opening stage

This second stage comes with the end of the first—sometimes gradually, sometimes abruptly, depending on the circumstances that affect the general partners individually and mutually. In this stage the couples begin to notice little things about each other, and those little differences began to annoy you. You feel bothered by some of those same things that were cute during the honeymoon stage. Reality sets in and concerns along with other obligations, including job, furnishing a home, raising children, and getting reacquainted with each other. Realizing that you married someone who is not perfect and even shows the undesirable qualities and traits may lead to some sober reflections on the theme: 'Wow, what happen to me . . .' Disillusion begin to set in. we start to realize that our spouse is not the perfect person that we had envisioned him or her to be.

This is a critical stage of the marriage and probably at its most vulnerable time. We realize that the expectations we had of the perfect marriage is not going to happen and we are hurt deeply by this disappointment. For some this realization is too heart quashing thus resulted in giving up on the marriage and usually end up divorcing.

Gloom Stage (Seven year itch)

Many of the young couples I counsel are in this glooming stage, they appear to be wondering with a gray cloud around them. I termed this stage the seven year itch because it seems to reach its peak between 5 and 10 year of marriage. In this stage couples have a hard time pleasing each other. The flame is almost out, you are running on the pilot-light and it is not starting every time. Romance and intimacy has become a duty rather than a pleasure. This gloom is a life storm and in order to get through it you will need to hold on to the rope and do not let fire go out.

Many couples stick with and try to work through their problems during the eye opening stage. They seek the counsel of family, friends, clergy, marriage, and family counselors. Some of these couples find the key they are looking for from these resources. Many others continue to tussle and their troubles get worse. Often the couples seek resolution through drug, alcohol or other addictions, and third party relationship in the form of extramarital marriage affairs. The gloom stage is where many couples find themselves considering a marriage separation or divorce.

Readjustment stage

This is the stage in which you not only recognize that your relationship can be more than it is, but also that you have the power to make real changes. You choose to become conscious and intentional, and begin a whole new chapter in co-creating the relationship you both dreamed of.

While one or both of you may continue to feel anxious, confused, afraid, and may resist making some of the changes, you take charge as partners of the direction of your happiness as a couple. And you do that best by taking charge of your own behavior. You start intentionally learning how to become the right partner. And, you go back to your list of values and of those 'ingredients' that you want to have in your marriage.

In this stage you realize that you're never going to agree with your partner on every issue. You may start looking for help by reading books, attending seminars and so on.

You learn to become more tolerant and forgiving. The atmosphere of the marriage changes from one of struggle and competition to one of co-operation.

Self-Actualizing stage

After several decades, the spouses are aware that at this stage they somehow managed to stay together and with that fact they are very pleased to continue until the end of their days. Acceptance of where they are in the relationship, others, and nature. Self-actualizing couples are not ashamed or guilty about their married nature, with its shortcoming, imperfections, frailties, and weaknesses. Nor are they critical of these aspects of other couples. They respect and esteem themselves and others. Moreover, they are honest, open, and genuine, without pose or facade. They are not, however, self-satisfied but are concerned about discrepancies between what is and what might be or should be in themselves, others, and society.

Recapitulating

While every union is unique, there are certain phases that most marriages go through. Each has the potential to either help a couple's relationship grow closer and more solid or to pull it apart. What's important to keep in mind that there is no perfect marriage and no relationship without conflict.

The stages outlined by the writer are in no way the law of "martial maturation" and are certainly not the only ones that have been hypothesized. However they do offer a common sense approach to planning your marriage

Gender Differnces . . .

Physically and mentally, the males and females are different.

When talking about the physical structure, the first thing that comes to mind is height and <u>weight</u>. Males are normally heavier, taller and stronger than females. It has been seen that males have large hearts and lungs when compared to females. In physical performance, the difference is typical.

A male is bolder than a female. The males perform any hard task, which a female cannot perform. And are generally heavier, taller and stronger than females.

Another physical difference that can be seen between males and females is the males have more bodily hair, especially in the chest region. Males have more collagen and sebum in their skin, which makes their <u>skin</u> thicker and oilier. When comparing the fat content, females have more fat percentage than males.

When talking about puberty, females have puberty changes about two years earlier than males. While fertility in females decreases as they age, especially after 35 years and it ending with menopause, males are fertile even in their old age.

Though the males and females have same brain weight when compared to their body weight, a male brain consists of about four per cent more cells 100 g more tissues than a female brain. It has been noted that males perform better in spatial and mathematical ability tests. On the other hand, females perform better in verbal ability and memory tests. While males have better long distance vision, females have better night <u>vision</u>.

When comparing the behavioral differences, males and females stand poles apart. While males are physically more aggressive, the females tend to be passive. A Male will take upon more risks than a female. Moreover, females are more emotional and express great intensity of emotion when compared to males.

What they say

Cambridge University psychologist and autism expert Simon Baron-Cohen:

> "The female brain is predominantly hard-wired for empathy. The male brain is predominantly hard-wired for understanding and building systems"

Writer and feminist Joan Smith:

> "Very few women growing up in England in the late 18th century would have understood the principles of jurisprudence or navigation because they were denied access to them"

John Gray, author of Men are from Mars, Women are from Venus:

> "A man's sense of self is defined through his ability to achieve results. A woman's sense of self is defined through her feelings and the quality of her relationships"

Sociologist Beth Hess:

> "For two millennia, 'impartial experts' have given us such trenchant insights as the fact that women lack sufficient heat to boil the blood and purify the soul, that their heads are too small, their wombs too big, their hormones too debilitating, that they think with their hearts or the wrong side of the brain. The list is never-ending"

In my research on this topic I came across the following article by *Michael Rucker*, posted on August 13, 2010.

"Most people are intrigued by the thought processes of the opposite sex. Despite rumors to the contrary, men and women *are* from the same planet. However, there are many differences between the brains of men and women. I have listed nine of them below. There is bound to be some respectful discourse about this topic, so please feel free to comment or provide alternative points of view below.

1. Brain size: The male brain is typically about ten percent larger than the female brain. Although the extra mass does give males more processing power, this doesn't make men more intelligent. Rather, science believes the reason for the increased brain mass is to accommodate the bigger body mass and muscle groups of the male (human).

2. Brain hemispheres: Many men are sharply left-brain dominant, while women tend to be more evenly balanced between left and right-brain processing. Women are therefore thought to be slightly more intuitive and sometimes better communicators. Men are often less socially adept, and are more task-oriented thinkers than females.

3. Relationships: Women are purported to have better communication skills and emotional intelligence than men. Women tend to be group-oriented, and apt to seek solutions by talking through issues. Men can have trouble picking up on emotional cues unless they're clearly verbalized—making for tricky communications between the sexes.

4. Mathematical skills: The inferior-parietal lobule, which controls numerical brain function, is larger in males than in females. On standardized tests, men often score higher on mathematical tests than women.

5. Stress: When faced with stressful situations, men usually employ 'fight or flight' tactics, while women use a 'tend or befriend' response that is rooted in their natural instincts for caring for their children and establishing strong group bonds.

6. Language: Women often excel at language-based tasks for two reasons: two brain areas that deal with language are larger in females, and females process language in both hemispheres while males favor a single brain half.

7. Emotions: Since women tend to have a larger deep limbic system then men, they're more in touch with their feelings and are better at expressing their emotions. This makes women better at connecting with others, but unfortunately also more prone to different types of depression.

8. Spatial abilities: The parietal region is thicker in the female brain, making it harder for them to mentally rotate objects—an important spatial skill. Women often report difficulty with spatial tasks, both on tests and in real life. Want to test this theory with a loved one?

9. Susceptibility to brain function disorders: Men are more likely to be dyslexic or have other language disabilities, since they're more often left-brain dominant. Males are also more prone to autism, ADHD and Tourette's Syndrome, while women are more susceptible to mood disorders like anxiety and depression".

There are also those believers who think that men and women communicate differently.

Differences in Male and Female Styles of Communication

Women are more likely to talk to other women when they have a problem or need to make a decision. Men keep their problems to themselves and don't see the point in sharing personal issues.

Women are more relationship oriented, and look for commonalities and ways to connect with other women. Men tend to relate to other men on a one-up, one-down basis. Status and dominance is important.

Women focus on building rapport, by sharing experiences and asking questions. Men like to tell and give information rather than ask questions. They share experiences as a way of being one-up.

If women have a disagreement with each other it affects all aspects of their relationship. Men can have a disagreement, move on to another subject and go get a drink together.

Women get things done at work by building relationships. Men build relationships while they are working on tasks with each other.

At meetings women nod their head to show they are listening. Men think the woman is agreeing with them. He then assumes the women will go along with his idea. He is surprised when she later disagrees, since she nodded her head. She has no idea why he thought she agreed with him since he never asked her.

At meetings, men only nod their heads when they agree. If a woman is speaking and she doesn't see his head nod as he listens, she assumes he either disagrees or is not listening.

Too often men and women see the differences between each other and make each other wrong, rather than appreciating how they can benefit from those differences.

The biblical account for this gender differences is to fulfill the roles in which God designed for each gender. Let us take a peep at the biblical roles for male and female:

God's Role for Male/Female

The Role of Men in God's Plan

By Mark Holden

This brief article is intended to give a brief overview of the Biblical picture of manhood. It is by no means exhaustive, and in fact could be greatly expanded upon in each of its parts. The purpose is to provide a quick overview that can hopefully whet the appetite for embracing deeper study of God's design for men and women.

LEADERSHIP—There is strong opposition today both in and out of the church concerning the Biblical teaching on masculine leadership. The overwhelming position of the Scriptures, both in teaching and in practice, is on the call to men to provide leadership.

Consider first of all the example of the fathers. Adam was created first, and in his primal position was given the responsibility to name the rest of the created beings. The realm of his jurisdiction included the naming of his helpmeet, which he first called "woman" and then later renamed as "Eve". God's instruction to the early couple was always directed to the man. It was Adam's responsible to impart to his wife and family the revelation that was shared with him.

THE PROTECTOR—Our Father protects us: simple but profound. And just like our Father, we as men have the responsibility to protect our families. To function as a husband is adhesive to function as a "house-band", the one who holds the house together.

Like it or not men, you and I have jurisdiction over the future of our children. Our faithfulness, or our sin, will have a direct effect on the lives of our children and the world in which they live. We can provide a shield of godliness and spiritual covering, or we can leave them vulnerable and entrapped by choices that we have made. In short, we are responsible.

THE PROFESSOR—When you hear the word "teacher", what image comes to your mind? Or even more revealing; consider the phrase "Sunday School teacher". If you see what I see then something of a feminine nature comes to mind. We generally consider teaching to be a women's thing. Women and children are sort of like peanut butter and jelly, they just go together, and we men get on with the real stuff of life, like work and play.

That is not the picture that is painted in the Scripture! The directive from God is that men be the teachers.

THE PROVIDER—The truths shared in this fourth section will be the most challenging for our culture to swallow. The reason for that is the reality that tomorrow morning a good share of our population will wake up and drive off to work in violation of this Biblical teaching. I also believe that this particular instruction is one of the most vital if our families are to be salvaged.

God designed man to work. His initial instructions to Adam were given to demonstrate his responsibilities in the garden. Because those instructions were given in the context of a perfect creation, yet untarnished by sin, it is evident that God intended for work to be good. It is a blessing to do Father's work.

As the Biblical narrative unfolds, it is also evident that God views the roles of men and women differently in relationship to work. In Genesis 3, which records Adam's sin and subsequent judgment, the curses that the LORD pronounces on the man and the woman are not the same. In fact they differ according to the life function of each of the recipients. For Eve the curse came in the realm of childbearing as well as her helpmeet relationship to Adam. Both of those life functions were designed to be good in their created purity; however they become burdensome under the weight of the curse. The fact that those roles are now burdensome does not change the fact that they are still the realm of the woman's created design and also that place in which she finds ultimate fulfillment and blessing.

For Adam the curse also was given in the realm of his life function. That very task that he was previously assigned is now made more difficult. It is still his realm, but under the curse he must work by the sweat of his brow.

The fact that differing life functions exist in no way implies that women are not expected to work, or that they do not work. However, their work is in a completely different realm than the work of men. Men are designed to be "field" workers. Women are designed to be "home" workers.

THE PRAYOR—Let's play another word game for a moment! I will give you a phrase and you picture the first thing that comes to your mind. Ready? "Prayer warrior". Okay, now be honest with me. What kind of person comes to your mind? Do you picture some saintly, elderly widow who suffers physically but radiates the presence of Christ because of her prayer life? Praise God for the prayers of faithful grandmothers.

Something is wrong though. According to God's leadership design, men should be the picture of prayer. I acknowledge that there have been, and are, great men of prayer. But we need a strong reminder that just as in other areas of life; men were intended to be the leaders in prayer as well.

The Biblical Pattern

"I will therefore that men pray everywhere, lifting up holy hands without wrath and doubting." (I Timothy 2:8) Paul's instruction to Timothy is not generic. He is not saying that "mankind" should pray. It is clearly an injunction to masculine people. Not only does the noun "men" identify that, but even more forcefully by the instruction that follows in verse 9 where Paul contrasts this admonition to men by saying, "In like manner also, that women adorn themselves . . ." It is very evident that there was a distinction of roles in the mind of the apostle. Christ's expressed desire through the hand of the apostle Paul was that men would engage in active prayer.

It is obvious that from the beginning the man was designed to be the intercessor. Cain and Abel made offerings to the Lord. Noah, upon leaving the ark, "builds an altar unto the Lord; and took of every clean beast, and of every clean fowl, and offered burnt-offerings on the altar." Job stood before the Lord on behalf of his family by rising early in the morning and presenting offerings on their behalf "according to the number of them all".

The Woman's Role in the Plan of God

God has a beautiful plan for womanhood that will bring order and fulfillment if it is followed in obedience. God's plan is that one man and one woman, of equal standing before Him but of different roles, should be bonded together as one. In His wisdom and grace He specifically created each for his or her role.

At creation, God caused a deep sleep to fall on Adam, and from him God took a rib and made a woman (Genesis 2:2 1). She was a direct gift from the hand of God, made from man and for man (1 Corinthians 11:9). "Male and female created he them", (Genesis 1:27) each different but made to complete and complement each other. Although the woman is considered the "weaker vessel" (1 Peter 3:7), this does not make her inferior. She was made with a purpose in life that only she could fill.

To woman has been given one of the greatest privileges in the world, that of molding and nurturing a living soul.

Her influence, especially in the realm of motherhood, affects her children's eternal destination. Even though Eve brought condemnation upon the world with her act of disobedience, God considered women worthy of a part in the plan of redemption (Genesis 3:15). "But when the fullness of the time was come, God sent forth his Son, made of a woman." (Galatians 4:4). He entrusted to her the bearing of and the caring for his own dear Son. The woman's role is not insignificant!

There are many books that are written and on book shelves that will provide you with an more in-depth information on gender differences. This author merely wanted to make you aware that as male and female there are significant differences so when you plan your marriage be sure to take them into consideration.

The final topic I will write about in this "Marriage Preparedness" chapter is *Financial Management"*. *According to one writer the five top reasons for marriage failure are (pay particular attention to the number 1 cause)*

Top 5 Reasons Marriages Fail

1. Financial Problems

For the most part, it is the lack of open communication about money problems that jeopardizes a marriage more than the financial problems alone. Everyone has financial issues concerning bills, debts, spending and budgets. How a couple deals with those issues can make or break a relationship.

2. Communications Problems

If a couple has communication problems prior to marriage, those problems are likely to get worse after tying the knot. It is important that both partners are able to discuss every aspect of married life openly and on a regular basis. A marriage without two-way communication will not last long.

3. Family Problems

Family relationships with children, parents, in-laws, siblings and step-children are all sources of marital problems. Raising children increases stress in the home and can cause minor differences of opinion to become major rifts in a relationship. Discretion is the better part of valor when it comes to family and marriage.

4. Sex Problems

Sex is an important part of marriage and the source of many marriage problems. Every marriage requires the act of consummation by sexual intercourse. Failure to consummate a marriage or problems with sexual frequency, quality, and infidelity are all common reasons for marriage failure and divorce.

5. Friend Problems

Close personal friends of either spouse do not always make the transition to friends of the marriage. Some relationships with friends can be toxic to the marriage if they insert themselves between spouses. A good friend will enhance a married couple's relationship. People who try to break a marriage apart are not quality friends.

All of these causes were addressed in previous chapters. However I wanted to show the relation between finances and the other four causes. It is my personal belief that we can change the position of finance in this comparative setting.

Finance is a common cause of friction for married couples, and it's no wonder.

Money is one of the major causes of friction in a marriage, and it's no wonder. Living in a world in which we are constantly worried about taking care of ourselves, it's easy to forget that marriage is a commitment to forge a new life with another person. The lack of trust emerging from society has created prenuptial agreements and separate bank accounts. These undermine the commitment to a shared life with a spouse and are contrary to biblical teachings.

There are five concerns that this occurs:

1. Couples do not receive Pre-Marital Counseling.
2. Couples do not disclose their personal finance status including debts and credit rating.
3. Couples do not develop a financial plan with goals.
4. Without a financial plan, couples do not work from a budget.
5. When it comes to money matters, couples do not effectively communicate.

Chapter 4 of this book addresses the five concerns in more details. The 30-years of my involvement with helping married couples with their marriage and family relations I can attest to the need for premarital planning. Research will support that those couples who received premarital counseling has a lower divorce rate.

The above chapter was written to provide couples seeking marriage a common sense guideline of expectations and pitfalls which occurs in most marriages.

Conclusion

The book is a holistic one where each chapter is critical to success. And because every marriage is different, each will struggle with different aspects of the book.

Some marriage have an easier time building trust than others but lack the discipline and follow-through to put processes and solutions in place. Others enjoy strategic planning and decision making but lose interest in repeatedly communicating their decisions to each other.

Whatever the case, couples must keep two things in mind if they are to make their marriages successful. First, there is nothing more important than making an relationship healthy. Regardless of the temptations to dive into more heady and strategically attractive issues, extraordinary couples keep themselves focused on their relationship's health.

Second, there is no substitute for common-sense. No amount of intellectual prowess or personal charisma can make up for an inability to identify a few simple things and stick to them over time. This book is written to alert you to those common-sense features that will enhance and enable your marriage to flourish.

A Culmination Word

Communities and nations will be transformed when men and women return to God and His purposes for them. God is looking for those who will dedicate themselves to standing «*in the gap on behalf of the land"* (Ezek. 22:30). He wants to bring His life-changing power to broken marriages, damaged families, shattered societies, and individual men, women, and children who need reconciliation with God and a restoration of His purposes for them. But He's waiting for couples like you. Genuine Christian Couples who will commit themselves to fulfilling their dominion purpose of spreading God's presence throughout the whole world. I pray that people will be able to look at your life and say, "Now I know what a genuine Christian Couple looks like," as they are renovated by God's presence in you.

Book Summary of *Married Couples Hierarchy of Needs,* by C.S. Gaffney

Main Topics:

- Hierarchy of Needs
- Communication
- Functional Needs
- Money Matters
- Parenting
- Common-Sense Marriage
- Marriage Preparation (Premarital Tips)

The hierarchy of needs are also present in married couples needs as well. Maslow's theory was focused on individual needs to survive in this high pressure society. However when you look at successful marriages there was some essential needs that were present and priortised in a manner similar to Maslow's theory on the hierarchy of needs.

In marriage the word communication is perhaps the most often used word during any counseling session. I have counsel with countless married couples and I feel safe to say that 98 percent of them mention the phrase, *"we cannot communicate"* or the other part of that **he or she will not listen to me**. On one of my assessment tools I have each member of the marriage to list the top five reasons he or she feel is the cause of their troubled relationship. The word Communication shows up in the five assessment areas of each member and very often at the top of the list. Why is there a perception that communication is the primary cause of marital relation problems?

As difficult as marriage can be to achieve, it is not complicated. And so, if I can't describe it in a page or two, then I've probably made it too complex. The true measure of a successful marriage is that it accomplishes the results that it sets out to achieve. To do that on a consistent, ongoing basis, a married couple must meet the five functional needs that are essential to a successful marriage. I am a great fan and follower of 'Patrick Lencioni" in is his book on the "Five Dysfunctions of a Team which align with my hierarchy of functional needs. I borrowed his model to further explain my functional of needs model.

Financial matter is among the leading causes of divorces especially in couples under seven years of marriage. In today's society many of the couples getting married are entering the relation as independent young adults who have accumulated personal properties, credit scores as well as debt. In most cases these issues are not reconciled prior to marriage. Trouble begins as infatuation wears off and realization sets in.

Marriage doesn't require special skills or best practice techniques to have a successful beginning. It does require that the relation is built on trust and strong physical and emotional bonds. Marriage can be as easy, or as difficult, as you make it. The key is to understand the simple and common sense of what makes a good marriage. I am not trying to minimize the complexity of marriage or indicate the simplicity of maintaining it.

Research show that couples who are getting ready for marriage spend numerous hours and lots of money planning the wedding but very little time preparing and planning the marriage. From my perspective the priorities are reversed. Marriage is for a life time and the wedding is a one-time special event. Logically thinking will move one to conclude that the event with the longest expectation would require the most effort. It is the discrepancy between the two acts that inspired the writer to focus on premarital preparedness. Specific areas to be discussed are listed below.